The Diary of Abraham Ulrikab

Text and Context

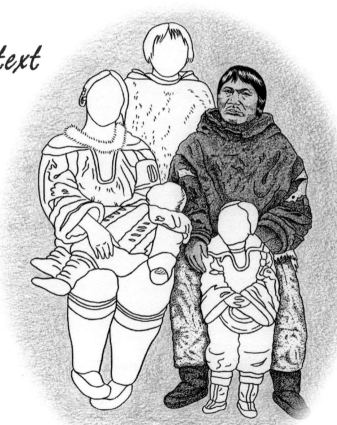

Translated by Hartmut Lutz and students from the University of Greifswald, Germany

Text © 2005, Hartmut Lutz
Photos © 2005, Hans Blohm, Assoc.
Cover art © 2005, Alootook Ipellie

The Diary of Abraham Ulrikab © University of Ottawa Press, 2005

Royalties will be donated to the Marg and Howard Adams
Scholarship

The University of Ottawa Press gratefully acknowledges support for
its publishing programme from the Canada Council for the Arts and
the University of Ottawa.

We also acknowledge with gratitude the support of the Government of
Canada through its Book Publishing Industry Development Program
for our publishing activities.

Library and Archives Canada Cataloguing in Publication

Lutz, Hartmut
The diary of Abraham Ulrikab : text and context / Hartmut Lutz,
editor and head translator ; Alootook Ipellie, preface and cover art ;
Hans-Ludwig Blohm, photos.

Translated from the German.
Includes bibliographical references.
ISBN 0-7766-0602-6

1. Inuit — First contact with Europeans — Newfoundland —
Labrador — Sources. 2. Inuit — Germany — History — 19th cen-
tury — Sources. 3. Ulrikab, Abraham, 1845?-1881— Diaries. I.
Ulrikab, Abraham, 1845?-1881 II. Title.

E99.E7L88 2005   305.897´1207182´09034   C2005-904911-1

Front cover illustration: Alootook Ipellie
Back cover and Appendix C photos: Hans-L. Blohm
Cover and interior design: Laura Brady, Brady Typesetting and Design,
www.bradytypesetting.com

University of Ottawa Press
542 King Edward, Ottawa, Ontario K1N 6N5
press@uottawa.ca / www.uopress.uottawa.ca

Printed and bound in Canada at University of Toronto Press

"A sense of 'racial ethics' should prevent us from displaying our equals in zoos."

"J.K.," 1880

Our translations are dedicated to
the Inuit People of Labrador

Contents

Foreword

By Alootook Ipellie

AT THE END OF January 1992, Iyola Kingwatsiak, an Inuk carver from Cape Dorset, Nunavut, was invited to participate in the Conference on Inuit Art held at the McMichael Canadian Collection in Kleinburg, Ontario.

Shortly after the conference, in the spring 1992 edition of *Inuit Art Quarterly* magazine, he was asked: *"What did you think about your trip to the McMichael conference?"* His reply: "I enjoyed being there, but the problem was that we sat there like pieces of art in a showcase display. The non-Inuit at the conference spoke as much as they pleased about their own lives and how they lived like Inuit. But they never gave us a chance to speak or asked us questions about our work. The white people dominated as usual. They think they are the experts and know everything about Inuit. This goes on all the time. I myself felt that the white people should be asking us Inuit what we think rather than encouraging the non-Inuit to talk about their childhood in our homeland. The only contribution I made while I was there was to do a bit of printmaking but,

again, the people who organized the conference didn't give us a chance to speak or respond to questions people might have had."

To the interviewer's follow-up question, *"Did you think that you were just there for people to look at you?"* Kingwatsiak answered: "You're very right about that. We're just like part of the show pieces; they treat us like carvings. The white people never seemed to be interested in talking with us. We work hard to make a living with our art and nobody asked us to talk about how we make our carvings and prints and what kind of tools and other things we use."

In the fall of 1880, eight Inuit from Labrador arrived in Germany, having been recruited by Adrian Jacobsen on behalf of his employer, Carl Hagenbeck, the owner of Hagenbeck's Zoo in Hamburg. According to one of the Moravian missionaries in Labrador the Inuit "were unable to refuse Herr Jacobsen . . . to be exhibited like wild animals outside in Europe to gain money . . ." with "promised daily earnings of three shillings per man, two shillings per woman, one shilling per child . . . the desire for European splendours is too strong . . ."

All summer Jacobsen had been travelling the coastlines of west Greenland and Cumberland

Sound off South Baffin Island before arriving in Hebron, Labrador looking for so-called "exotic" peoples still practicing their traditional cultures on the land and the sea. His main objective was to recruit Eskimos to be shown at the "Volkerschauen" or "peoples shows" that provided ethnographic shows of different cultures. Three years previously, in 1877, Hagenbeck had successfully exhibited a group of Inuit from Greenland. Now he wished to duplicate that success with Abraham and the seven other Inuit in the entourage – on the one hand, Abraham's family of five Christian neophytes and, on the other, Terrianiak's shaman pagan family of three.

The voyage from Labrador across to Europe on the Atlantic's rough seas must have been a curious one. These two groups did not see eye-to-eye, as their daily lives led them on different paths – one family, devout Christians who prayed daily and left their future in the hands of the Lord; the other, "heathens" who were very much in the hands of the natural world and still practicing their "magic" to the very end. But they were heading to Europe for one mutual reason: hired by Hagenbeck as live human exhibits to demonstrate their survival techniques as "primitive" hunters and gatherers on the Arctic lands and waters to audiences, large or small, in different European cities. They had had enough of carrying heavy debts and experiencing great poverty. The trip to Europe gave them a glimpse of a financial windfall that would certainly wipe out their financial predicaments this side of the Atlantic. It seemed a win-win situation, so they hopped on board the ship with encouraging optimism in their hearts.

In reading the contents of Abraham's diary and letters published in these pages (translated from the original Inuktitut to German and then finally to English) one feels empathy with the author. He and his fellow travellers must have gone through a myriad of emotions from the day they decided to join Jacobsen on the voyage to Europe, through the five months on exhibit, to the moment their eyes closed for the last time from the ravages of the smallpox they all contracted within days of one another.

As Iyola Kingwatsiak said, "I enjoyed being there, but the problem was that we sat there like pieces of art in a showcase display." All these years after the passing of Abraham, nothing fundamental has changed in the human condition of his fellow Inuit and the so-called "civilized" peoples of the world. Whether displayed in a zoo or an art gallery, Inuit people are still treated as exotic specimens.

Acknowledgements, or "habent sua fata libelli"

(EVEN) SMALL BOOKS HAVE their fates or histories, so I would like to share the "fateful" stories that went into the production of this little book, in order to acknowledge and thank those who helped to make it a reality.

In 1987, when visiting Canada for the first time on a Faculty Enrichment Grant from the Canadian government, I met Newfoundland scholar Dr. Robin McGrath in London, Ontario. She was most hospitable and generous with her time and knowledge, and she gave me several books by and about Inuit authors, including Elizabeth Goudie's *Woman of Labrador*. She also gave me a copy of geographer J. Garth Taylor's pioneering article, "An Eskimo abroad, 1880: his diary and death," about the visit of the eight Labrador Inuit to Europe, published in *Canadian Geographic* in 1981. Taylor's article contains several passages of Abraham's diary translated into English by

Dr. Helga Taylor. This article was the first and only English language contribution on the subject available at the time. Although there was literary scholarly interest in the text, it was hampered by the language barrier. But Abraham's diary was "known." In the two earliest books in Canada documenting the history of Inuit literature, there are quotations from and references to Abraham's diary as the first autobiographical text by an Inuit author: Robin McGrath's *Canadian Inuit Literature* (1984)[1]

---

1. Robin McGrath's pioneering (doctoral) study *Canadian Inuit Literature: The Development of a Tradition* (1984) is even today the most informative introduction to Inuit Literature in Canada up to the Eighties. McGrath also edited anthologies of Inuit literature and published scholarly articles on Inuit writing. In her dissertation, McGrath speculates about the existence of early Inuit manuscripts in obscure archives and then draws attention to Garth and Helga Taylor's discovery and translation of Abraham's diary:

"One hears, when traveling in the Arctic, that the French Oblates, the Moravians, or the anthropologists at Laval, have attics full of manuscripts and diaries, fiercely guarded by octogenarian keepers, but all these reports cannot possibly be true or all Inuit over the past two centuries would have to be employed in scribal activities. There may, however, be some grain of truth in the myth.

The earliest extant diary by an Inuk that is known was found only a few years ago by J. Garth Taylor among a collection of 80,000

and Penny Petrone's *Northern Voices: Inuit Writing in English* (1988). Apart from these two scholarly studies, nothing seemed to be available in English about this "episode" in Moravian missionary history that produced this earliest Inuit autobiographical text.

Back in West Germany, I wrote to the Moravian archives at Herrnhut, then in East Germany, and received copies of the Moravian letters about the trip (Herrnhut is a Moravian centre, and in German, the Moravian Brethren are called "Herrnhuter"). Later, in 1988, at the opening of a Canadian Inuit photo exhibition at the University of Osnabrück, West Germany, brought to us by Walter Larink

from the Canadian Embassy in Germany, I spoke about Abraham and the Inuit group from Labrador, and I speculated that this, and similar stories slumbering in missionary archives, would provide good research topics for German students graduating in English. The next morning, one of the students who had been present at the opening, Renate Jütting, came to my office and told me she had decided to write her teacher's diploma final thesis about Abraham's diary, and she wanted that topic reserved for her. We agreed, and she later went ahead with determination, stamina, and level-headed intelligence. She obtained from the Moravian Archives in Bethlehem, Pennsylvania, a photocopy of the "Sütterlin" hand-written German translation of the diary, and, years later, in 1994, she also gained the copyright for an English translation. Her final thesis, *Das Tagebuch des Abraham als Beispiel erster Inuit–Literatur* ("The diary of Abraham as a first example of Inuit Literature," 1991) provided some of the historical background for the introduction to this book. To date, hers is still the most comprehensively researched and documented study about Abraham's diary and its historical context, albeit in German. Later plans by Renate Jütting and Gundula Wilke to

---

pages of documents in the archives of the American province of the Moravian Church in Bethlehem, Pennsylvania. The author, Abraham, was one of eight Inuit who visited Europe in 1880 and, when all the native members of the party died of smallpox, Captain J. Adrian Jacobsen sent the diary and the other personal possessions of the Inuit back to Labrador. When the diary arrived at the mission in Hebron, it was translated from Inuktitut into German by a missionary, Brother Kretschmer, and both documents eventually found their way into an uncatalogued bundle of reports on early Labrador missionary journeys.… and the English translation of the Kretschmer manuscript, which was done by Dr. Helga Taylor, gives some fascinating glimpses of the life the Labrador Inuit led." (McGrath, 4)

bring out a bilingual edition of *Abraham's Diary* in English and German in the OBEMA series (*Osnabrück Bilingual Editions by Minority Authors*) unfortunately never materialized. However, we felt throughout that the story ought to be told, and that the materials should be published in English, preferably in Canada. A letter about this plan, years ago, to the Inuit Tapiirisat in Ottawa was never answered, and a renewed attempt in 2003 with Inuit Tapiriit Kanatami also failed.

In the summer of 1998, I had a chance to visit Happy Valley–Goose Bay in Labrador and meet Doris Saunders, the founding editor of *Them Days* Magazine, which specializes in local (oral and written) history. I told her about possibilities of translating Abraham's diary for *Them Days*, and she expressed her interest. In the summer of 2002 at the University of Greifswald's Institute for British and American Studies, I offered a senior seminar, entitled "Translating, Publishing, and Editing a Marginalized Voice, *Das Tagebuch des Abraham*, into English." The students and I decided to translate into English all German sources available to us, and to try to have them published in Labrador. For our translation we used Renate Jütting's photocopy of the original

manuscript of Brother Kretschmer's translation of Abraham's diary. All participants worked on translations of the diary and related texts, and in smaller work groups the students conducted research on Inuit autobiographical writing, on Hagenbeck's *Völkerschauen*, on Rudolf Virchow's *Völkerkunde*, and on contemporary newspaper articles about the visitors from Labrador. Some of the letters had to be transcribed from the old Sütterlin style German handwriting into modern writing style to provide an accessible text, which students could translate for this book. None of the students were ever trained in the skill of reading Sütterlin, but I had received a brief introduction to this writing style in elementary school half a century ago, and I had privately tried to keep up this seemingly obsolete cultural skill. Thanks to a consultation with my colleague, the historian Werner Buchholz, we were able to decipher and transcribe even Kretschmer's least readable letter. The Greifswald students worked with great enthusiasm and steady perseverance on the project, which lasted well beyond the semester into the summer break in July and August. While we were working on the research and the translations, I was in email contact with Doris Saunders, who received the manuscript and, despite health problems and many other commitments, began entering it into her system. Then, quite unexpectedly, *Them Days* suddenly decided against the publication and returned the manuscript to us.[2] Whatever *Them Days'* reasons may have been for abandoning this project I would like to thank Doris Saunders for her commitment and for at least having tried.

The hope of having our translations published in Canada had been a major motivational incentive for the students' commitment. To curb their disappointment, I told them that I was confident that we would eventually have the translation published somewhere else in Canada – to have our gift delivered by having Abraham's diary returned to its origins, a project I firmly believed in. But at the time I had no clue as to the If, the How, and the Where of making this optimistic prognosis a reality. A year later, however, thanks to some very supportive nominators, things began to fall into place when I unexpectedly won the 2003 John G. Diefenbaker Award and came to the Institute of Canadian Studies at the University of Ottawa for an entire year of research – thank you Wladimir Krysinski and Anne Brisset, Chad Gaffield, Parker Duchemin, Peter Kulchyski and Stephen Scobie!

Putting together a book, I have been told, is a bit like having a child. You feel responsible for it and you are likely to suffer from postpartum depression once you have finished the manuscript and have to let go. But midwifery it seems is alive and well, not only in Europe. When in the spring of 2004 Denis Renaud published a short note on my research projects in *Initiatives*, the bulletin of the Institute of Canadian Studies at the University of Ottawa, he mentioned that I was looking for a publisher for Abraham's Diary. Obviously, the bulletin does find its readers. Ruth Bradley-St-Cyr, Director of University of Ottawa Press, read that request and said "That's me!" She understood the potential of Abraham's story and became enthusiastic about publishing our translation. I am so grateful to Ruth for her commitment, her optimism, her professional competence, her encouragement and good

---

2. Copies of our translation were, however, given to outsiders, as I later learned through Dr. Rainer Baehre, historian at Grenfell College, Memorial University at Corner Brook, Newfoundland, who is doing research on Virchow, and who provided me with valuable information and materials, which I hereby acknowledge most gratefully. *Habent su fata libelli*, indeed!

cheer, and I am sure our baby is in good hands.

Since she contacted me about the manuscript things have gone quite smoothly, and more people and connections just fell into place. After coming to Canada's capital in February 2004 I met, for the first time in my life, three Ottawa residents I had known about before but had never met in person. Now, they have all became contributors to this book project in different ways, and I would like acknowledge and honour their help by telling the stories.

Since first seeing some of his artwork and reading some of his texts, I have always admired Alootook Ipellie's outstanding poetry and prose. Moreover, his drawings and sketches have always impressed me by their meticulous craftsmanship and their creative and often tongue-in-cheek humour. Prior to coming to Canada I had even dedicated an article about the Abraham Diary to him and Robin McGrath (Lutz, "Unfit…"). Less than a month after my arrival in Ottawa, Alootook and I were introduced to each other by Hans-Ludwig Blohm. We became friends, and now Alootook Ipellie has contributed a preface to this book and an illustration for its cover.

Maybe three months before my departure to Ottawa, I received a letter from a professor at Carleton University who had learned about my being at Greifswald University from a newsletter put out by the German Embassy in Ottawa, also announcing the Diefenbaker prize. Roger Herz-Fischler, an expert on the history of mathematics, had asked the archives of our old library – Greifswald University was founded in 1456 – for certain materials on Adolph Zeising, a 19th century German intellectual who researched and wrote on the golden number. The electronic transmission of the materials had not worked, and with the help of the chief librarian and student Andrea Mages, who had been part of the Abraham translation project, I was able to bring him the copies he needed. Meanwhile, his book *Adolph Zeising: The Life and Work of a German Intellectual* has come out, and Roger and Eliane Herz-Fischler, my family, and I have spent some wonderful times together as friends. It was Roger Herz-Fischler's research on Zeising's studies in phrenology that opened my eyes to the ideological and historical links between the neo-classical obsession with the ideal proportions of the human body according to Greek and Roman sculptures and Virchow's racist investigations.

About a month before my departure for Ottawa, I received a phone call from a lady whose accent was clearly from my North German home region. "Am I speaking to professor Hartmut Lutz?" – "Yes, that's me." – "Did you just win the Diefenbaker Award to do research on Canadian Aboriginal Literature?" – "Yes." – "And are you going to Ottawa?" – "Yes." – "And you were born in Rendsburg?" – "*Jau*," I said in our Schleswig-Holstein *Plattdütsch*. – "Well," she responded also in *Platt*, "I'm from Rendsburg, too, and so is my brother. He lives in Ottawa. He is a photographer, and he loves the North and its peoples, and he has done a book on the North, which we have just translated and published in German. I'll send you a copy. You must get together. A last question: Were you a boy scout?" – "No, *Jungenschaft*." – "That's even better! *Tschüss*!" A few days later I received the beautiful book, and by now, Hans-Ludwig Blohm, the arctic photographer from Rendsburg, and Ingeborg Blohm, the painter from neighbouring Büdelsdorf, and myself, have become fast friends who can speak *Plattdütsch* together in Ottawa. Hans-Ludwig Blohm has donated some of his outstanding photographs of Moravian remnants in Labrador for our book.

I am moved by and grateful for Alootook's, Roger's, and Hans-Ludwig's input to this book, and even more so for their friendship.

Finally, I would like to thank the many people, named in this introduction or unnamed, who have supported *Abraham in Context* in one way or another. The authors' royalties will go to the Marge and Howard Adams Scholarship Fund for Aboriginal Students, and my greatest thanks go to Renate Jütting and my patient Greifswald students, who by the time of publication will all have graduated, but whose commitment will be remembered in the context of Abraham Ulrikab's and his companions' fateful venture 125 years ago – to whit:

Claudia Albrecht
Dorothea Buchholz
Karen Ebel
Jennifer Felkel
Kathrin Grollmuß
Nadine Hiepler
Karin Hinckfoth
Jana Jerchel
Sabine Ihlow
Martina Lange
Andrea Mages

Axel Nieber
Jana Schnorfeil
Susanne Rumpoldin
Verena Sachse
Anja Weidner
Susanne Zahn

Hartmut Lutz
Ottawa
January 2005

Nakvak Fiord, 2002.
© Hans-L. Blohm.

Introduction

*By Hartmut Lutz with Renate Jütting
and Ruth Bradley-St-Cyr*

ON AUGUST 8TH 1880, the schooner *Eisbär* (polar bear) sailed into the port of Hebron, the Moravian mission station on the coast of Northern Labrador. The vessel's owner was Adrian Jacobsen (1853–?), a Norwegian sea-farer, collector, and trader of ethnographic artefacts and human specimens, who was traveling for Carl Hagenbeck, the founder and proprietor of "Hagenbeck's Thierpark," the Hamburg zoo named after him. This was not Jacobsen's first voyage across the North Atlantic. Three years earlier he had visited Greenland and, with the consent of the Danish authorities, had hired, vaccinated, and then transported a group of Inuit and their belongings to Hamburg, where they were exhibited and performed seal hunts and sleigh rides for thousands of visitors at Hagenbeck's Zoo. In May the following year, after "Hagenbeck's Eskimos" and their artefacts had been on display in Paris, Brussels, Cologne, Berlin, Dresden, and Copenhagen, they had returned to their Greenland homes, all sound and wealthy, having earned a total of 600 crowns.

By contrast, Jacobsen's 1880 voyage had begun with drawbacks and disappointments. In the North Sea ferocious headwinds had impeded his progress. Then the ship had encountered an unusual calm in the North Atlantic. In Greenland, Danish authorities had resolutely refused to allow any Inuit to travel with Jacobsen, not even for his scientific ethnographic purposes. The woman who had travelled with him to Europe in 1877 "cried every day" because "she was not allowed to come along," according to Jacobsen, and he privately cursed the Danes for keeping the Inuit at home for their own purposes, to keep them hunting. "It is a shame that one tyrannizes the Eskimos in this manner," he complained. The best Jacobsen could manage to get was some supplies, two kayaks, and some sickly dogs in the hopes of finding Inuit from elsewhere to travel back to Germany with him.

After Greenland, the *Eisbär's* attempts to reach Cumberland failed because of heavy ice and day after day of fog. Time was running out. By the time the ship reached Hebron, Jacobsen was desperate. His journal relates these worries: "From the first day I boarded this ship I have had worries as never before… now nearly all my courage is gone, my expectations diminished, and my heart yearns to return… I can expect only ruin on my return." Upon reaching Hebron, Jacobsen must have been frustrated and all the more eager to finally meet with success. But even here the German speaking Moravian missionaries, who were friendly and hospitable enough, were absolutely opposed to letting any of their Christian flock travel with Jacobsen to be exhibited like zoo animals or to be exposed to the lurking moral and spiritual dangers "outside" the mission in Europe. "To undertake such a journey to Europe is seen to be synonymous with leading them to their doom," complained Jacobsen. "It is sad that a people are so suppressed, and still more so that Europeans demonstrate such power."

Jacobsen did manage, however, to hire as a pilot and translator a 35-year-old Inuit man, Abraham, the husband of 24-year-old Ulrike, father of four-year-old Sara and baby Maria. Abraham Ulrikab (his last name being derived from his wife's name) accompanied Jacobsen to the Northern Hudson Bay Company post at Nakvak, just north of Ramah. Their guide was a very accomplished man, well liked by the missionaries for his eager intelligence, his contribution as a violinist in church, his penmanship, his language and drawing skills, and his work ethic. Abraham was in debt to the missionaries to the tune of £10 but had refused to rely on their alms box. So, he needed money.

In Nakvak there was a small settlement of "wild Eskimos" (Inuit traditionalists who had refused to be Christianized). When the *Eisbär* arrived on August 19th most able-bodied Inuit had left Nachvak to hunt caribou further inland, and only a few people had stayed behind, mostly elders and children. But with the help of Abraham's powers of persuasion, Jacobsen managed to hire the shaman Terrianiak, who was about 40, and his wife and fellow shaman Paingo, whose age was given in a range between 30 and 50 years, as well as their teenage daughter Noggasak.

After this initial success, Abraham also let himself be persuaded by the local Hudson Bay trader, Mr. Ford, to disobey the missionaries, and to join Jacobsen's enterprise. So, on their return to Hebron, ignoring all Moravian protests, Abraham, Ulrike, Sara, and Maria, as well as Ulrike's nephew Tobias, boarded the *Eisbär* and, on August 26, Jacobsen with his

"It is said that 1500 people (namely Eskimos) belong to the parishes of their mission stations. There are six mission stations. The most southerly is Hopedale, then Zoar, Nain, where the superintendant lives, and north of it comes Okak. The name Okak means cod. Then flows Hebron and the most northerly is Ramah."
— *Jacobsen's Diary*
Photo by Hans-L. Blohm.
Map © Labrador Inuit Association Office, Nain.

KILLINEK 1902

OKAK 1776

RAMAH 1871

HEBRON 1818

KAUK HARBOUR 1770

NAIN 1771

ZOAR 1865

NISBET'S HARBOUR 1752

HOPEDALE 1782

MAKKOVIK 1894

NORTH WEST RIVER 1960

HAPPY VALLEY 1954

eight Inuit guests, and many artefacts he had taken from grave sites near Hebron, immediately set sail for Hamburg. He had to postpone vaccinating the Inuit until arrival in Germany as there were no doctors in Labrador. There he fell ill and was hospitalized, and vaccination of the Inuit was again neglected – a fatal omission.

The crossing was rough for the Inuit, who suffered from seasickness, especially the children, and most especially Noggasak. When their schooner was anchored near the mouth of the Elbe River, which would take them to their destination of Hamburg, a violent gale drove them east towards the shallow coastal waters off the northern province of Schleswig, threatening to run the ship aground. Jacobsen, in his halting German, relates in his diary how he suddenly heard some loud yelling, and he rushed on deck, fearing somebody had gone overboard:

> Here I was presented with a curious spectacle. The heathenish Eskimo Tiggianiak stood at the fore, gesticulating with his arms, and giving forth one howl after the other – I thinking he had suddenly gone insane. We all stood around him and nobody knew what to do with him, his voice louder than the storm's…
>
> Then one of the other Eskimos came forward and told us to leave him in peace, because he was now working magic, magic for good wind – at the same time his wife came and made the most wonderful movements with her hands. After he had howled his witchery formulas he walked calmly towards his cabin, promising that we would have good wind soon. A few hours later we indeed had good wind, and Tiggianiak, who is said to be known as a great magician in his home, insisted that he had done it himself (meaning that he had called the north wind). I was happy in my soul that the fellow had not gone crazy in the process, as I had believed in the beginning. Our sailors, however, from that moment on, were convinced that Tiggianiak was a real sorcerer, because the wind had turned from blowing from the southwest towards blowing from the north. (transl. H.L. from Jütting, 21)

Ufubaf mit Familie.

Carl Hagenbeck, frontispiece from his memoir
Von Tieren und Menschen: Erlebnisse und
Erfahrungen, *published by Vita Deutsches Verlagshaus,*
Berlin, 1909.

Ufubaf and family: the family from
Greenland who preceded Abraham's group.
Photo published in Hagenbeck's memoir.

After their arrival in Hamburg on September 24th, Jacobsen took sick, being hospitalized and bedridden with fever and diarrhoea for weeks. Hagenbeck hired Adolph Schoepf from Dresden, who worked in Hamburg as an impresario, to organize the shows and to accompany the Inuit. In addition, Frau Jacobs – who so often accompanied groups for Hagenbeck that she was known as "Ethnic Mother" – was hired to cook and do laundry for them. The employees from Labrador were put on display in Hagenbeck's zoo, where they demonstrated such skills as harpooning, dog-sledding, and paddling their kayaks. On October 2nd the group took the night train to Berlin, where they stayed in the zoo until November 14th. Winter came unusually early that year, and the Inuit began suffering from the humid cold, developing runny noses and headaches. Jacobsen, who had somewhat recovered, again joined the group. At one point, however, he whipped Tobias for some misdemeanour the nature of which we don't know.

Throughout, the baptized and the pagan Inuit families were kept in separate huts, which imitated their earth lodges back home. The Moravians had asked Jacobsen to keep the two groups apart, so that their neophytes would not be contaminated by Terrianiak's heathenism, which might cause them to backslide in their religious beliefs, and besides, the general public, and particularly those involved in the fledgling *Völkerkunde* (ethnology) expected to observe in the "civilized" Christians from Hebron a behaviour and a level of accomplishments superior to that of the "wild Eskimos" from Nakvak.

While they were in Berlin, the Inuit had many visitors, including some very welcome ones for Abraham and his family – their Moravian Brothers and Sisters in Germany. As well, they attracted the interest of and were examined by Germany's foremost physician of the time, Dr. Rudolf Virchow, then president of the Berlin Ethnological Society, who tried to establish their exact "racial identity" between "Mongolians" and Greenlanders. On November 7th, Dr. Virchow gave a talk on his findings. As well, some 16,000 people had visited their show in Berlin.

Jacobsen later accompanied his wards southeast to Prague, which was then part of the Austro-Hungarian Empire. They arrived on the evening of November 15th. "There our Eskimos were in the Kaufmanns Menagerie," he reported. "The working hours for the Eskimos were 11-12, 3-4, and 6-8." The group remained in Prague until November 29th. They then crossed to Germany's southwest and travelled to Frankfurt (November 30th until December 12th) and neighbouring Darmstadt, were they were scheduled to stay for only three days. The stay was extended, however, when Noggasak died on December 14th. Physicians had consistently failed to diagnose her symptoms as smallpox, attributing her illness to a "sudden stomach ulcer."

The day after Noggasak's burial on the 16th, the group was taken north to Krefeld (December 17th to 28th), near the Dutch border. The week leading up to Christmas was ceaselessly rainy and depressing, but the Europeans tried to cheer their Inuit guests with a Christmas Eve party. Jacobsen was responsible for the details:

> Mr. Hagenbeck had asked me to buy various Christmas presents for the Eskimos. The dining hall was made available to us and there we had a very nice Christmas tree which we decorated, and when all was ready we let the Eskimos come in. They enjoyed them-selves very much and were entertained as much by the tree as by the presents. These gifts consisted of underwear, a fiddle for Abraham and a guitar for Tiggianiak. Also each family received a large group photograph which had been taken in Prague. We had wine brought in and remained together until 11 o'clock, never suspecting what a cruel blow fate held in store for us.

On Christmas Day the cruel blow came when Paingo suddenly fell ill. The symptoms were the same as Noggasak's. "We called for a doctor at once (Dr. Jacoby), who assured us that it was only rheumatism and we need not worry." But the next day "little Sara also fell ill, complaining of chills and vomiting." The day after that, Paingo died. Jacobsen was astonished at the turn of events, saying "We had been with her 10 minutes earlier and the doctor examined her and assured us that it was not dangerous."

The depressed survivors took the train to Paris where news of Sara's death reached them on New Year's Eve. On New Year's Day, Jacobsen arranged for the others to be vacci-nated against smallpox, but preventive measures proved to be too late. Between January 7th and 16th, all of the remaining Inuit died in Paris – Maria, January 7th; Tobias and Terrianiak, January 9th; Abraham, January 13th; Ulrike, January 16th. All these deaths took place in the St-Louis Hospital where Jacobsen had also been admitted for a relapse of his fever. Jacobsen was devastated and wrote, "Did I really have to drive these poor brave people to die in a foreign country? How has it come to pass so differently from my intention? In the beginning it went so well; we had just learned to know and love one another."

We know from Jacobsen's diary and Dr. Virchow's report that Noggasak was buried in Darmstadt. But what became of the remains of those who died in Krefeld and Paris? Hospital undertakers in Paris would have buried the bodies soon after death, but their burial place is unknown. From Jacobsen's unpublished diary we know that the medical doctors in Krefeld, intent on finding the cause of Paingo's death, did an autopsy on her. Her illness, had originally been attributed to rheumatism. Jacobsen, for reasons unknown, had Paingo's skullcap given to him at the autopsy. After all the other Inuit died he passed it on to a professor from the museum in Paris.[1]

---

[1] Seen in (callous and cynic) materialist economic terms, the Inuit group had a high exchange value, which totally collapsed and collided with the loss of use value at the moment of their deaths, unless use could be made of their remains. This misuse of the body or parts of the body of deceased "exotics" in museums and freak shows seems to have been widespread, not only in Europe, as the following examples may serve to demonstrate.

The body of the father of Minik, the New York Eskimo, was discovered embalmed and on display in The New York Natural History Museum [Cf. Kenn Harper. *Give Me My Father's Body: The Life of Minik, The New York Eskimo* (New York: Washington Square OP, 2000)].

The embalmed and mummified body of Monsieur Edouard Beaupré, "The Willow Bunch Giant," was discovered in a garage in Quebec [Cf. Ron Revard and Catherine Littlejohn. *The History of the Métis of Willow Bunch* (Saskatoon: © Ron Rivard and Catherine Littlejohn, 2003).]

In my private edition of Alice Walker's novel *Meridian* (1976), which includes an "ethnic freak-story" in its own right, there is a glued-in newspaper cutting from *Frankfurter Rundschau* (presumably 1987?), about two Inupiat bodies from Alaska, who were discovered mummified in a cave eighty years ago, and who were now being returned to the Inupiat for internment. They had been exhibited at fairs and shows for eighty years. The article mentions Wesley Cowan, curator of a Natural History Museum in Cincinnati, and David Stone, Mayor of Point Hope.

In the poem "Julia" by Hopi-Miwok poet Wendy Rose there is the persona of the "lion woman" Julia, who was exhibited by her own husband as the "ugliest in the world," and who gave birth to a hairy baby who died six hours after delivery. When Julia died, her "loving" husband had her stuffed and continued to exhibit her body. [Cf. Wendy Rose, *Bone Dance: New and Selected Poems 1965-1993* (Tucson & London: U of Arizona P, 1994), 60-62.

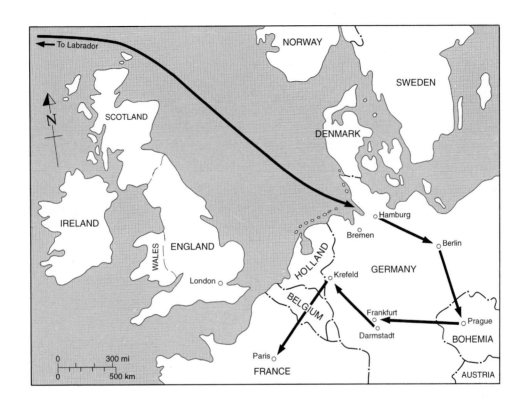

The route taken through Europe by Abraham and his companions.
Map by William Constable, Constable Enterprises Inc. © 2005.

The story of the eight Inuit from Labrador in Europe presents one of many shameful and depressing episodes in nineteenth century German (and other Europeans') history with regards to colonial and missionary contacts overseas. It is marked by economic greed and exploitation, by ignorance and prejudice, by scholarly and popular curiosity, and by callousness and racism. But there were also instances of Christian compassion and humanist concern, and there were attempts by both the Inuit guests and some of their European hosts, to meet as contemporary human beings on a person-to-person level. Their story might have been forgotten, like those of so many other victims of colonialism and racism, had not one member of the group, Abraham – perhaps inspired by Jacobsen's diary keeping – kept a short diary of the trip. Unfortunately, the original text in Inuktitut, which was shipped to Hebron, is lost and we do not even know whether Abraham wrote it in "Sütterlin" (old German handwriting), in Latin letters, or in syllabics. However, there is a 14-page handwritten translation of Abraham's diary into German by Brother Kretschmer, a Moravian missionary who had served in Labrador. There is other documentary evidence as well: entries in Moravian diaries, letters between Moravian missionaries, newspaper reports, and Dr. Virchow's academic article. All of these documents were available in German only and thus remained closed to the majority of the Canadian public, including possible descendants of relatives of those two families who were taken to Europe from Labrador over a century ago. The following translations will allow readers to follow the journey of Abraham and his companions. With this publication their story can finally be told, for the first time, in English.

Glossary

There were different spellings for these Inuktitut names and many different variations were used, as can be seen from the many newspaper articles about the visit:

Abraham Ulrikab: Abraham, Ulrike's husband

Noggasak: Noggasack, Nochasak

Paingo: Bairngo, Paieng

Terrianiak: Tigganick, Terrianniakat, Tiggianiak, Tareganiak, Tereganiak

Kablunat = white people

Nachvak, Nakkwak = Nakvak

Netsuk = seal

MORAVIAN PEOPLE AND TERMS:

Brother Kretschmer = missionary in Labrador when Abraham left for Europe

Brother Elsner = missionary formerly in Labrador; in Germany when Abraham visited Germany

Herrnhuters = Moravians

Mission des Brudergemeinde = monthly newsletter of the Unity of Brethren

Teachers = missionaries

UAC = Unitäts Ältesten Conferenz (United Elders' Conference)

Hebron, Moravian Mission, 2002.
© *Hans-L. Blohm*

The Diary of Abraham Ulrikab

STANDING: *Tobias, nephew of Abraham and Ulrike (18??–1881)*
SITTING: *Ulrike (1856?–1881) and Abraham (1845?–1881)*
CHILDREN: *Maria (1880–1881) and Sara (1876?–1880). Zeitschrift f. Ethnologie (Anthropolog. Gesellsch.) Bd XIII Taf. XIV, W.A. Meyn Lith. Verlag von Paul Parey in Berlin.*

My dear teacher Elsner!

I write to you, because I'd like to tell you the following. We are greatly sad. When they brought me to Europe, I probably totally ignored it at first, but then I prayed to the Lord continuously that He might teach me, if it really was a mistake, because I believe in all His words. But because I was in deep misery, I often prayed to God to help me to free myself from this and to hear my sighs, because I even wasn't able anymore to take care of my relatives, which I was usually able to do, even when I

LETTER FROM THE HEBRON CONFERENCE TO UAC, AUGUST 16TH, 1880

A schooner with a German flag entered our port to our astonishment on August 10th. It was a Mr. Jakobsen from Hamburg who is traveling on behalf of Hagenbeck, the menagerie owner, and is looking for antiquities etc. but at the same time also for Eskimos in order to exhibit them in European cities. Originally he had wanted to get heathens from Northumberland but could not reach the coast because of the huge amount of drift ice so he came to us

did not believe in my Lord and Saviour yet who died for me. In different kind of ways we have been lured, but even all this I didn't recognize. But as I was in doubt to pay all my and my late father's debts from kayaking, I thought (at this chance) to collect some money for discharging them. I also believed that I might see you. Then I thought: Our way is destined by the Lord. We all cried a lot, my wife, I, and our relatives; but none of them wanted to hold us back. This way we took our decision before the Lord. Not that we would have been tired of

from there within nine days. We resolutely explained to him that we neither are allowed nor willing to help him so that our christened people are exhibited outside and looked at like wild animals for money. But he could not share our reservations and could not see why we did not want to be useful in the interest of science, since the Eskimos would be generously rewarded like the people from Greenland, whom he took with him three years ago. In spite of our resistance it would have been accomplished and one family had already agreed. But, because he did not want to take only four but eight to ten people with him, it

our teachers, but due to the weight of my debts, of which I still have 100 Shilling. I didn't want to act like a fool, but I remember to have wished to see Europe and some of the communities over there for a long time. But here I wait in vain for someone to talk about Jesus. Until now we only saw reckless people in our house. We pray that the Lord may help us here and everywhere we will travel to with our show. I admonished my relatives that they above all do not forget Jesus. We didn't expect that! Such recklessness is not our pleasure. I thought we would see

did not happen and he will now try the Nachvak region. However, we would like to know how to behave in cases like this.

Kretschmer, W. Haugk

A. Hlawatscheck

P.S. The Eskimos' contribution to the mission £ 2.12 s. 4 d.

AUGUST 20TH, 1880

DEAR BROTHER CONNOR

Now something quite new and special. The vessel "*Eisbär*" (Polar Bear) from Hamburg, which was here recently, returned from Nachvak yesterday and got only one family

you very soon … Once we have been to church, in a big community in Berlin. (Because of that) we have been feeling happy until late night; yes indeed, we didn't want to go to sleep. The Lord seemed to be with us for a long time. Even as we went through the streets we sang praises and were astonished. And it became clear to us how well we were taken care of in our country, yes indeed, long and great are the blessings we receive, yes indeed. [. . .]

Mr. Hagenbeck has done much good to us: he gave us beds and a violin and music to me. Now we will travel to

from there. Now, however, one family from here decided to go along after all, the married couple Abraham and Ulrike (brethren in the Lord's Supper). I told them that we absolutely cannot allow our baptized people to be exhibited like wild animals outside in Europe to gain money. They could not, however, understand our reservations, did not want to upset us, but were unable to refuse Herr Jakobsen. In addition, the promised daily earnings of three shillings per man, two shillings per woman, one shilling per child. That will make quite a lot, if the promise is kept and they would return next year with a payment and

different cities; therefore pray for us, especially when we are in Catholic countries. We will suffer a lot from homesickness. We will go to Dresden, Paris, England, Herrnhut, Petersburg, and Vienna, if it's true what they say . . .

I will have faith in God here in Europe that nothing bad will come across; that even the evil people, who surround us all the time, can't harm us.

The wife of the Northerner is sick, very sick indeed. We are very grateful that they have a home for themselves. We don't like their habits, both practise magic.

presents. I told them that we did not in the least begrudge them to see so many beautiful and great things in Germany, but that we had to despise this way towards the goal. But no Eskimo can understand that it should be bad for him to receive pay from somebody who wishes to see him. Moreover, the desire for European splendours is too strong, and besides, Abraham intends to see all Labrador-missions and the congregations Herrnhut, Niesky and [...]. In any case, you will be informed from Hamburg about their arrival. Since we were entirely opposed to this, we neither could nor would sign a contract with

I often ask them to convert, but it doesn't help. Again and again they catch a bad cold. They reject to take any medicine; they hope to get well by magic. We often suffer from colds, too, are often sick in Berlin and are very homesick and miss our land, our relatives, and our church. Yes indeed, we had to learn from our mistakes. I don't fear; I will be disadvantageous to our people (after our return). Far be it from me to do so. Already now I know better about many things, especially also that the commodities have to be brought to us on a

Herr Jakobsen. Therefore, we are not responsible for any good or bad consequences that may still occur. Jakobsen regretted not to have bought anything before in [*Northall?*] village (he had not even wanted to come to Labrador but to Cumberland). Now, however, there was no time. I briefly asked him not to give them any alcoholic beverages and to supervise them so that they may not see anything evil etc. This morning he sailed away with them, very happy not to have made the voyage in vain. Last night an unmarried lad reported that he should and would go along as well. He also went along this morning, and is of an auda-

long way, which in fact has to raise the prices, and that the journey our teachers have to go on is very dangerous. Yes, we wonder that teachers long to come to us poor people, whereas we already had enough of one sea voyage!

The food here is no good. We don't lack dry bread; we also get some fish. Because of the fish we take some refreshment.

We thank you very much for writing to us. At this moment we probably don't lack anything physically. We all

cious character, anyway. But they are free people and we cannot hold them.

Without doubt the dear brethren and friends in and outside the congregation will be rightfully indignant when it is made public in the newspapers that Eskimos from Hebron are exhibited publicly in the zoos of Berlin, Dresden, Paris. We can attest, however, that while it is happening with our knowledge it is entirely *happening against our will*. To excuse the Eskimos it must be stated that they cannot understand our reservations against the trip; they are upset that we could not say yes, but it is too much for them to let go of all the pleas-

send many greetings to you, your relatives, and all believers at yours. We often see you both in mind and my wife sends her regards to your wife Bertha in the Lord. However we are, wherever we may be, we don't want to run away.

Abraham, Ulrike's husband

(English translation, based on German text, as published in *Missionsblatt der Brüdergemeinde*, No. 12, December 1880.)

ures and riches hoped for. Last winter Abraham and his family suffered great poverty and would still not be helped from the alms box. Next winter he will be in for the same since he gained very little in spring and could not repay his debt of £10. Therefore, he now wants to be given money in Europe for a net so that he can then repay his debts. He also wishes to see Herrnhut, Niisky and Schalke [?] together with his wife, and Herr Jakobsen has promised him this. Should he really make it there, we would like to ask you not to treat them in any repulsive manner as disobedient ones etc. which would do more harm than

Diary of the Hebron Eskimo Abraham
about his stay in Europe 1880

In 1880, the family Abraham Ulrike was taken to Europe by Mr Jacobson, the agent of H. Hagenbeck. With them the unmarried Tobias, also from Hebron, as well as the heathen family Tirrianniakat from the North. All died in Europe. Abraham's diary was sent back to Hebron together with some other things. There it says:

good because they would only think that we begrudged them the good luck to see so much beauty. We would like best if they could be spoken to by brethren from Labrador (Abraham is personally known to Brothers Kern, Elsner, Linder, Sister Erdmann). He plays the violin, the clarinet, the guitar, under- stands a little English. His wife Ulrike, aged 24 years, a well-behaved person, was never excluded, served for four years with us as housemaid, a good pupil with Brother Erdmann, knows a little German.

The heathen family from Nachvak were planning to move to Rama next winter to be

In Berlin, it is not really nice since it is impossible because of people and trees, indeed, because so many children come. The air is constantly buzzing from the sound of the walking and driving; our enclosure is filled up immediately.

It was not until the 22nd of October that we heard that the *Harmony* had arrived, when two acquaintances from Hlawatschek came to us. They were two teachers (missionaries), and they were so happy when they saw us that they knew us immediately and called our names, told converted. The man is called Terrieniak (fox), the woman Paingu (homesickness), the child Nachosak, about whom you can read in the diarium of Rama for the year 1876. Eventually, we shall learn next year whether these people or ours were considered alike, whether a difference was observed between the baptized and the heathen. The fact that the Eskimo knew that Greenlanders were in Germany three years ago also added much to make such a visit desirable, and, had the ship stayed longer, many more would have registered to go along, because they are children and suspect no evil but always expect the best.

us to sing, and because there were some things we were not [...] they were very happy and even thanked us greatly and invited us to their house and their church. We really want to, either, but are not able to, as there are too many people. Indeed, going out by daytime is impossible because of all the people, because we are totally surrounded by them, by many very different faces.

✳

ON OCT. 23RD, snow was falling all the time, the Kablunat are freezing; even we are freezing very much.

Shouldn't it be good if some of this were made public in the *Herrnhut?* [Moravian magazine] Please act according to what you deem best. May the Saviour protect them in the world and may He let serve for the best even this crooked way. We fear they will be difficult people for us afterwards, but even in this, His will be done.

Best wishes to you and all
Your dear colleagues
Your humble brother
B.G. Kretschmer

Norddeutsche Allgemeine Zeitung—Berlin

Abraham, Tobias and Terrianiak Demonstrate a Seal Hunt

☞ The Eskimos started their show on Sunday in the *Zoologischer Garten* to massive applause from an audience of almost 7000. The most interesting part of the show is probably the seal hunt. In it, Tobias plays the seal to be hunted, wrapped in furs. As soon as Tareganiak spots him, he drops to the ground, imitating the sound of a seal, crawling towards him. Finally the animal is in firing range, the rifle thunders, the seal is hit and the hunter jumps up cheering, ties a leash he has brought with him around the body of the shot animal, and trails it to the hut where wife, kids, and friends await him. Tobias and Tareganiak play their roles with great enthusiasm, and Tobias patiently lets himself be trailed along the ground as the shot seal. The hunt on water is just as interesting. The kayaks of the Labrador Eskimos differ enormously in construction and handling from the Greenlandic boats. All Eskimos present here, especially Tobias and Tareganiak again, play in these harpoon hunts of seals, salmon, and seabirds; further they go on sledges pulled by dogs and show their talents at snowshoeing – all of which highly amuse the audience.

No. 487, Oct. 18th, 1880

Tobias' Fondness for Children*

A visitor of the *Zoologischer Garten* tells the 'K. J.' how fond of children the Eskimos already are after having been here for only two days: Among the curious people coming to the Eskimos on Monday were also very many children, who tried to communicate with the Eskimos by language and gestures. It was already getting dark and the spectators had left, and also the Greenlanders had gone into their huts. Only Tobias, the 21-year-old, not absolutely unhandsome boy, sat outside leaning against a tree, and he was surrounded by a group of boys and girls, who joked with him and asked many things. A little, maybe 10-year-old boy with a pretty, always smiling face found the special favour of the northern son, who petted and caressed the clever boy for every comment. He might have touched the boy a little rough; the boy pretended crying and Tobias jumped up at once, put the boy's head on his chest and covered him with kisses. When the boy looked up again, laughing heartily, Tobias joined him laughing after a while and caressed and kissed the boy again. Almost by force the Eskimo had to be separated from the cheerful children, and only after the leader of the group indicated that he will see the children tomorrow again, he said goodbye to his Berlin friends for the day and retreated into the hut.

**Nr. 492,
Oct. 21st, 1880
(Morgenausgabe /
morning edition)**

How the Zoo's Polar Bears Fear the Inuit Guests, Whereas the Inuit Fear the Lions and Tigers*

The Eskimos put the polar bears of the *Zoologischer Garten* – which has always been a place of tranquillity – in truly hot excitement. As soon as an Eskimo comes close to its cage, it bursts to the bars in loud grunts and tries to break through them to attack his natural enemy, who he recognizes despite the long captivity. The Eskimos also cause uproar among other animals in the house for beasts of prey, but it is hard to convince them to enter it anyway, because they cannot overcome their natural fear of lions and tigers.

Samples of Inuktitut Language*

In general, the Eskimos have already settled here and especially the young Tobias made many new friends, welcoming them with a friendly *iltarnemek* (hello). *Kamutik suicksak* (sledge ride) gives him the biggest pleasure. Very fast he follows the *Kingmiks* (dogs) with his 20 foot long *Herautak* (whip), of which you can hear the *Schiknbuk* (cracks) very far. Abraham prefers *Nankatorit* (boating) to the sledge rides. Tereganiak is not fond of work at all;

he prefers devoting himself to philosophical contemplation: "*schilalok obleme, kaugbot schilake, kangsabot Sonntag, innuit onuktut!*" (Bad weather today, good weather tomorrow, the day after tomorrow Sunday, many people then!), he told his fellow yesterday; and even one not knowing the language could hear how the thought of the excitement caused by each Sunday terrified him. The language of the Eskimos from Labrador differs substantially from that of the Greenlanders. The Labrador Eskimos do not seem to have any songs from their native country; when singing they use German tunes which have been translated into their language, like: "*Jarit dreissig inkasat, atik ulikatigi vagit*" (You are already 30 years old and have survived many storms.)

**Nr. 496,
Oct. 23rd, 1880
(Morgenausgabe/
morning edition)**

The Inuit and the Stereotype of the "Dying Race"*

☞ The Eskimos from Labrador, who are now presented to us at the *Zoologischer Garten*, are relatives of a rapidly dying people. All missionary stations of the Herrnhuter are populated by only 1100 Eskimos after the last census. The population of Hoffenthal alone has decreased by 18 in the last six months. Only a few children survive to the 6th year. In Nakvak, home-town of the heathen Tereganiak, there are only 11 families – about 40 people — left altogether, another heathen settlement counts about 100, and a third one about 40-50 inhabitants. One can almost predict the year when the people of the Labrador Eskimos will be entirely gone from earth.

**Nr. 501,
Oct. 26th, 1880
(Abendausgabe/
evening edition)**

* *Translators' titles*

✢

ON OCT. 25TH, we saw teacher Kern and one of the great teachers (Dewitz), who send out teachers.

✢

OCT. 27TH. Storm and rain. Yesterday on the 26th, we went to church, and prayed and sang together. We were all very greatly cheered, also all our Kablunats, very greatly we have been inspired. We people sang together in the church, "Jesu ging voran" ("Jesus led the way"), we also spoke the

UAC MINUTES, OCTOBER 21ST, 1880

For a few days now an Eskimo family from Hebron is in Berlin, whom an entrepreneur has won over and brought to Europe to exhibit them here in different cities. Belonging to the Hebron parish, they let themselves be won over for this purpose in spite of all the warnings from the missionaries. After all, however, they insisted on being allowed to visit different parishes. It means a lot to Br. V. Dewitz in Niesky to visit this family, when he gets a

Lord's Prayer. The assembled were greatly inspired by our voices. And again, we were recommended pleadingly to the Lord. And again, there was choir: "Wir stehen getrost auf Zion fest" ("We rely confidently on Zion"). Then we were at a loss because of all the blessings, even the Kablunat, too. When the choir had finished, the man at the table called upwards, then the trumpets started playing; "Kommst Du, Jesu, vom Himmel herunter auf Erden" ("Come ye, Jesus, down from Heaven to Earth") and other melodies. When we had finished we were given an enthusi-

chance on his travel to Berlin to a missionary feast next Saturday, like he says in his letter from October 20th. To this end he asks the UAC, whether a retired missionary from Labrador, for instance Br. Kern in Berthelsdorf, could not be requested to go to Berlin and maybe accompany him (Br. v. Dewitz). UAC agrees to this and Br. Kern should receive the invitation. Miss. [...] agreed to cover the expenses. Br. Kern was asked immediately after the meeting and is willing to take on the task.

The 23rd of October 1880 in UAC
Read and approved.
E. Reichel

astic welcome, our hands were shaken greatly. Before the table we sat.

After this event, the teachers often appeared in our house (in the zoo) and sang (and prayed); even women who came into our hut have joined in the singing and recommended us greatly to Jesus.

One day in the evening, us wearing big coats and shoes, we went to see things (the wax works) exhibited in a large house, we drove there (sitting) in a house. When we arrived, we went in and saw many people gathered there, —

BREMEN, NOVEMBER 10TH, 1880

DEAR BROTHER REICHEL!

You will be surprised to get a letter from me again. But, as I think I already told you, I wrote to the Eskimos in the "Zoologischer Garten" in Berlin, gave them our admonishing, serious, and many consoling words since I could not doubt that they would be terribly homesick, since after all, they are natives from Labrador! Finally, yesterday the responding letter came from Abraham, who used to be my ward. I immediately translated it in order to send it to you.

but – they only looked like people; they looked so much like real people that you did not notice anything. Yes indeed, some of them even took breath, and some were moving, and all kinds of things, indeed, to name all is impossible. We also saw Napoleon's wagon, it had been brutally snatched from him during the war. And all sorts of rifles, indeed, manlike, of great variety. Nubians, Africans we have also seen, and Chinese and Indians and Americans and Californians, yes indeed, the inhabitants of the earth, very many did we see in Berlin.

Yesterday evening I gave a short oral report about the situation of these Eskimos in our local Christian Men's Association, as far as it is apparent from Abraham's writing. [...] The situation of these poor beguiled Eskimos moved the Men's Association very much. I was asked a lot of questions whether I could travel to Berlin before they would be dragged along to Petersburg or to Paris.

The matter stayed undecided.

Arrived at home, I got 40 Marks as support for the journey to Berlin, so I could not help but see the journey as coming from the Lord.

Magdeburgische Zeitung

The Eskimos in the Zoological Gardens of Berlin

☞ Thursday, October 21, 1880. Morning-Edition (No. 493)

As stated in the public announcements, the Eskimos from Labrador and Greenland began their "presentations" last Sunday.

But, what are these curious, small and stunted human figures from the forbidding North presenting?

Well, undoubtedly the first thing they have to offer is that which intrigues us "middling sons of this earth" (daughters included, of course) the most – namely, themselves.

And thus we have arrived at a point which, however, does not reside within the field of anthropology proper – which has received so much attention recently, and which, of course, means "knowledge about the human" in German – but which, seen from another angle, may well belong to this new field of knowledge after all.

Of course, we will most meticulously avoid taking issue in any way with these gentlemen belonging to the anthropological type. They must make their observations and conduct their measurements undisturbed; they must construct all thinkable and unthinkable lines and angles on the faces and skulls of Eskimo-individuals, and must assess in exact numbers the relationships among the former. Somewhere, in the filing cabinets of science, there must be a tiny compartment that has not yet been crammed quite full. One has to hurry up, therefore, to produce the necessary tabulations. But even for the filing cabinets of science there is a point in time when, as in the administration of the courts, the destruction of accumulated files is ordered, to make room for the new, which, in turn, and after a predetermined length of time, will be met by the same fate. If it continues following within the same ruts, the scholarly filing cabinet, section "Anthropology," will soon contain an alarming amount of stuff. Everything is recorded; each tiny fragment of a shard, each little peg of wood, each splintered piece of rock is kept. All of a sudden there is an "anthropological museum," and even a very "interesting" one. Today, whenever something manages to establish itself as being "interesting," it has won the game. We are inclined to exclaim in the words of that profound Prince of Denmark: "To be interest-ing – that is the question!" This is the condition we have to reckon with most seriously, because it is of such unconditional and unavoidable pertinence. Truly, the word of Dr. Faust is valid even in this matter: "Behold this sign, to which they bow, those black hordes." And the whites no less! "It is interesting!" Against this fact there can be no logic, no objection, no questioning. It is interesting to be able to watch the stage-set life and the antics of these beings that have been brought from their home in the snowy drifts. Because, that's what it really is, and what it will remain forever. Just look at the little people a little more carefully, a little more in the proper sense of "anthropological," and you will realize immediately that there is a melancholy expression especially on the faces of the Eskimo women. They know fully well that they are being exhibited, exposed to the curious, prying glances of old and young. Who knows what these children of the roughest North may be thinking about their highly educated European fellow humans!

Too bad one has to be reminded of it! One could have almost forgotten it when faced with that "interesting" anthropological play-act. And it would have been pardonable enough, since, not far away, the East-Indian pachyderms, the thick-skinned elephants, are romping about within their spacious and firmly built enclosure, where you can observe them in their natural existential expression (behaviour). And here you may likewise observe those northwestern bearers of thick furs in their natural existential expression (behaviour), romping peacefully, as is their way, inside their huts that are only fenced off by a wooden wicket. And it is beyond telling how "interesting" they are! Because those Northerners walk around just as we do. However, in their sealskin clothes they may seem a little clumsy to us, and a bit like bears. But who knows how we may appear to them? Yet, it is after all very interesting to see how the Eskimo mother carries her little child on her back in her hood. Maybe that is why the hood is cut in such a large and ungainly fashion. Maybe, it is only for the sake of the head of the mother, who may perhaps need the protection of the hood against the all too cutting cold. In -40 Reaumur [-50 Celsius] degrees and more, even Eskimos will occasionally feel a little uncomfortable. And now for traveling on water in that narrowly pointed boat, in which the Eskimo sits, and knows how to propel his vessel with a rather primitive paddle. The boat even floats on the water. It is gigantically interesting! And whenever the Eskimo father wants to give his family the pleasure of a little voyage, he takes his little boy on his lap and lets his wife stretch out long on the narrow boat. As you have noticed, they are now all three in the boat, and again that is very interesting. And now for throwing the spear at the imagined fish-enemy — it is almost like going on manoeuvres, also against an imaginary foe. But the crown of all things interesting should be reserved for the sleigh-ride in a wooden chassis covered with reindeer skins and drawn by eight dogs.

Now we would maintain that nothing is gained by the most meticulous observation of all these "interesting details," even when seen from the so-called anthropological point of view. Neither our education nor our knowledge have been expanded or deepened in any way. We cannot, however, and nor can many others, suppress a feeling of embarrassment about these recently proliferating "human exhibitions," and especially about "human exhibitions" in zoological gardens! There is the species "lion" in its different degrees, there is the family of pachyderms, there is the species "monkey" in its countless variations. And now one is adding the "species homo," as they were recently called in a daily newspaper, in manifold degrees. We have already had opportunity to see Nubians, Negroes, Lapps, Patagonians, and, undoubtedly, other "interesting peoples" will also send us their representatives. Or rather, our animal traders on their extensive travels will now and again be able to find some "humans" who will suffer themselves to be persuaded to co-operate. And we do not want to interfere with anybody's "trade." While someone may travel the world in the company of tightrope walkers, with singers or virtuosi, others may travel with "interesting foreign people." Anybody may do as he pleases. But in our opinion one should not try do demonstrate the idea that there is only a gradual difference between all the species, in this graphic way of treating human beings like exhibition pieces in zoological gardens! In our opinion this business in human exhibition pieces has something decisively repulsive. We cannot shake off the idea of the slave trade. Surely, this may not be the case at all. But to bring these "Menschenkinder" (human children), these images of God, if we may say so, to bring them right into the middle of zoological gardens as exhibition pieces, seems to be absolutely incompatible with science and our knowledge about humans and the essential being of humanity.

We are totally prepared to have our opinion smiled at and ridiculed as sentimental by some. Nevertheless, we have wanted to express it here. If these "interesting" human specimens need to be exhibited at all, a sense of "racial ethics" should prevent us from displaying our equals in zoos. It should be easy to identify appropriate localities elsewhere.

Berlin, October 20th

J. K.

All Sundays there were violin concerts in front of us, in a great house.

Our fellow men, the fox family (Terrianiak) stopped to be cheerful, because they are tired of the people. And we in the other house have been very patient, although we have also been greatly tired. Constantly in the evenings, we pray, wanting to be helped. This thing (our praying) also seems to achieve something within us.

Some Kablunat some (Catholics) [...] laugh at us, but this did not make us tired, as their souls are also to be

Since however, according to today's report in the *Börsenzeitung* [financial newspaper], this will be the last week of the Eskimo's stay in Berlin, the matter suffers no delay if it is to be achieved at all, and I therefore have decided – God willing – to depart for Berlin tomorrow morning, praying that the Lord may give His

blessings to this journey. [...]

The local pastor really wanted to include the letter of Abraham in the local church paper.

Until now I have been evasive, so that if the article is published at all our papers will not print it later than others, since many religious

laughed at. To some of them, who were talking about us, I have even given answers often, as they could speak English. Some of them were even horrified by our Northlanders often. Every day I have consistent work drawing people, Labrador and Nain.

✤

3. NOV. We heard that many ships sank at Heligoland and London because of storm.

✤

and political papers like to republish what is printed in the *Bremer Kirchenblatt* [church paper in Bremen]. After my return from Berlin, however, I will not be able to avoid the inquiries any longer.

With heartfelt regards to you and the request to likewise give my regards to the dear brothers of the UAC. I remain yours truly [...] Brother

A.F. Elsner

[Source: Moravian Archives at Herrnhut, Germany, R 19 Bf. 16b]

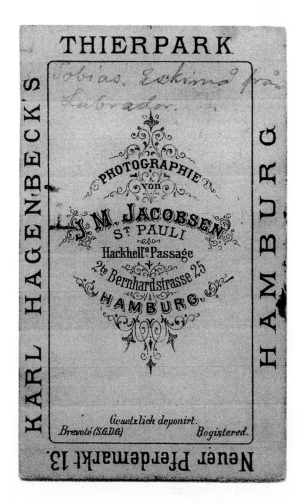

Souvenir card (front and back) of Tobias from Hagenbeck's Thierpark in Hamburg. From the Kenn Harper Collection.

7. NOV. Had sorrow again. Our companion, the unmarried Tobias, was beaten with a dog whip by our master, Jacobsen. Mr. Jacobsen was immediately furious because, as he said, Tobias never obeyed him and had got himself into trouble too often. He was nearly not taken and sent away. If Mr. Jacobsen does that twice I shall write to England as I am told. Afterwards, he was very friendly towards me so that I don't write. Even our two wives were immediately bought silken ribbons. If Tobias is frequently as stubborn, he won't get paid, but if he is nice, he will get greatly paid. After this incident, Tobias was very sick.

EXCERPTS FROM *Missionsblatt der Brüdergemeinde*, NO. 12, DECEMBER 1880

With the Eskimos in the "Zoologischer Garten"

It was a peculiar deeply moving after-celebration of the missionary feast in the Berlin Hall of Brethren, when we one day later – 8 brothers and sisters in number – on Monday, in the morning of the 25th Oct., visited our "brothers and sisters from Hebron" at the "Zoologischer Garten" in Berlin. Dr. Kern, known to the readers of the newsletter as former Labrador-missionary, and I went there on a special order of the mission-department. –

The pond on which we kayak around is very cold; we always have to get rid of the ice first before we can kayak. At times there is a great cold. We also saw the animals of the Berliners, fish, a seal [...] and nearly all kinds of sea animals. Meat (of seals) we miss very greatly, let be, some of it is probably not very good, but that's what we mostly eat: coffee and rusk in the morning, codfish, potatoes, beer and ship bread for lunch. Coffee and bread at 4 p.m. herring, beer and bread at 6 p.m. The Kablunat audience always take delicious things with them to treat us with; all

Yes, there they came; Abraham in a hurried run when he saw his old teacher, then the youth Tobias, then Ulrike, wife of the first mentioned, with her little, cute, only 11-month-old Martha and the 4-year-old Sara; soon the heathen approached us: Terrieniak (fox) and his 50-year-old wife Paingu (homesickness); the daughter Nochavak (young caribou) appearing a little later, with long pendants of pearls in her ears like her mother. We shook hands in a friendly manner with all of them; with shining eyes our Christians especially welcomed Dr. Kern, to whom Abraham had already sent a letter a day before.

kinds of things to chew, which they give to us, and big fruits, which have even juice. On some days I have also demonstrated outdoors, as the Kablunat wished it so greatly, even if I am not very good at it they don't mind.

I was constantly told to write my name, occasionally, there very many voices, one always took it away from the other, to please them all was impossible, there were too many.

✡

"The great teachers are sending us to you" – that is about how Dr. Kern turned to Abraham in their language – "They are very sad that you have been so foolish to come here, it will not do you any good, but now you are here, and so they send you their best regards as our brothers and sisters, and admonish you to walk as Christians and to remain faithful to the Saviour!" And similarly they kept on talking to them. After the first joy, there was a look of embarrassment on Abraham's face; maybe he expected to hear a fiercer word of reproach. But what should be the use of it now? Now it was important to win their trust, and to show

10. NOV. It was snowing greatly, even in Berlin.

Daily we heard the voices of the canons very loud. But it is very easy to get sick with a bad cold; I am still quite well, although I have a badly running nose. But the daily work is getting hard due to indisposition, because our child Sara is ill, and because we all have to suffer; that is certainly difficult. That (Sara) has to stay is regrettable, but she herself is not reluctant, because she is already able to understand that it can't be any different.

them that the love of the German brothers and sisters is with them. Soon the characteristically childish – and if I may say so – honest expression returned on his wide face, and he assured us that they already realized they had been foolish, and to tell the great teachers that they would not look at evil things crossing their ways, and that they would ask Jesus for letting them keep the faith. For this moment it was meant seriously. We were also delighted to hear that Abraham takes care of his family, and together with his fellows gives morning and evening blessings every day. The Eskimos have a hymnbook, a Bible and a Daily Textbook

Sometimes we are given some money, sometimes two pence, sometimes one mark, sometimes 50 pence, sometimes 20 pence, also cigarettes every day. It is too long until the year is over because we would very much like to return to our country, because we are unable to stay here forever, yes indeed, it is impossible! It buzzes and roars day and night because of the rattling of the sleighs and the constant voices of the steam whistles.

When we were travelling with steam, we were faster than flying. We always used such places as grand gentle-

with them. It was a moving moment when we eight brothers and sisters gathered with our Christian Eskimos in their housing, a reconstruction of their native huts; and when they were singing in their language and we finally stroke up together in both tongues the verse: "Die wir nun alle hier zusammen sind" ("Now that we are all together here"). We spent about three hours in their enclosure and managed to talk about more things, while they had to present their arts in going by kayak, on a sledge and other things several times in front of the audience. We have to keep silent about other details. […]

men are wont to use. The train was so long that there was a great distance between both ends. We were in the middle in a very nice house (wagon), we could not close the windows in order to see, looking out was impossible because of the wind; my eyes were bad and swollen with seeing, although I hardly stuck my head out [...].

I think it is my duty to correct possible wrong opinions and to acknowledge in gratitude at this moment, that the physical and mental well-being of the Eskimos is cared for in liberality and with great effort. We were lucky to meet Mr. Hagenbeck in person, who had just arrived this morning to meet with the interests of these people. Not only is he concerned to care for the appropriate food of the Eskimos – regardless of the possibility of personal losses for himself – but also for the moral well-being of them. That is why the Christians and the heathen live in separate huts; alcoholic beverages are strictly kept away, and as far as

[Brother Kretschmer crossed out the following passage in square brackets, perhaps with an eye to readers in Europe. It is also possible, however, that it was crossed out in the original.]

[While we were travelling, our countryman Fox (Terrianiak) worked magic quite exceptionally, although he was in the beautiful steam wagon, he was extremely distraught by his witchcraft and couldn't smile at anyone, when we arrived.]

✣

possible it is watched for continuous activity, by their preparation of food, by all kinds of sewing and wood carving works and such things. An experienced, clever agent of Mr. Hagenbeck is around the Eskimos all the time for supervision, and he had promised to inform our Dr. Kern in writing in necessary cases. In every respect we met only with the most endearing and most profound obligingness.

Much to our delight we heard from the director of the "Zoologischer Garten," Dr. Bodinus – who was also present – that we were given the generous permission to pick up our Eskimo brothers and sisters for a meeting in

Neue Preussische Zeitung

Abraham's Artistic Accomplishments*:

☞ **Berlin.** In the *Zoologischer Garten* Abraham Paulus of the Eskimos especially draws the attention of the visitors. He is seen as the most educated of his fellows. Shortly before his departure to Europe he mapped the coastline of Labrador with its many bays and courses of rivers upon his own journeys. The sketch of the map is currently in the hands of the director of the *Jardin d'Acclimatisation* in Paris who wants to present it to the Geographic Society there. Abraham is also very skilled in drawing figures. Among others he did his self-portrait in watercolors, an achievement that, clumsy as it may seem, would nonetheless satisfy higher expectations in regard of likeness. Abraham also plays the violin, writes, and reads the language of his country.

No. 249, Oct. 23rd, 1880

*Translators' Title

The Eskimos!

Hurry up Berliners, small and tall,
to the *Zoologischer Garten,*
where real Eskimos are waiting for you,
ready with fish oil!
They are a nice and cosy people,
tousle-head like –
The man, the wife, the little brat,
they take what they can get!
But while they still walk around
in raw caribou furs,
the **Goldene 110**
is offering the following selection:

Over 8000 paletots and Kaiser coats now only half-price (almost give-away, no one beats our prices with real goods) for only 5, 6, 7, 8 to 9 thaler and for very exquisite showpieces for 10, 11, 12 thaler. 6000 very exquisite English fall suits, the noblest for parlor and promenade (whole suit) now for only 4, 5, 6, 7, 8, 9 to 10 thaler, showpieces for 11, 12, 13, 14 thaler. Trousers and vests: 2½, 3, 3½, 4½, 5, 5½ thaler. Prime quality. Black suits of 7, 8, 9, 10, 11, 12, 14, 15 thaler. Prime quality. ☞ 8000 dressing gowns for cut-down prices of 3, 4, 5, 6, 7, 8, 9 thaler. Prime quality. ☞ A huge stock of reduced winter paletots and dressing gowns will be given away for as good as free.

« Erstes Deutsches Vereins-Magazin"
(Goldene 110)

110	Leipzigerstrasse 110	110

Please look closely for house number "110"!

No. 250, Oct. 24th, 1880

Mrs. Ulrike!

Mr. Abraham and Mrs. Ulrike,
the Eskimos from Labrador
feel very odd
with fur and lance here in Berlin!
Ulrike just said to her spouse:
Your sealskin coat is out-of-fashion,
the apron suits you terribly –
I'd like to see you as a dandy!
And Abraham chivalrously
went to the **Goldene 110** immediately,
cried out "Ei jong gni" seeing all the throwaway prices
and put his bags full of:

Over 8000 paletots and Kaiser coats now only half-price (almost give-away, no one beats our prices with real goods) for only 5, 6, 7, 8 to 9 thaler and for very exquisite showpieces for 10, 11, 12 thaler. 6000 very exquisite English fall suits, the noblest for parlor and promenade (whole suit) now for only 6, 7, 8, 9, 10, 11 to 12 thaler, showpieces for 13, 14, 15, 16 thaler. Trousers and vests: 3, 3½, 4½, 5, 5½, 6, 6½ thaler. Prime quality. Black suits of 8, 9, 10, 11, 12, 14, 15, 16, 18 thaler. Prime quality. ☞ 8000 dressing gowns for cut-down prices of 4, 5, 6, 7, 8, 9, 10 thaler. Prime quality. ☞ A huge stock of reduced winter paletots and dressing gowns will be given away for as good as free.

110	"Erstes Deutsches Vereins-Magazin" (Goldene 110)	110
	Leipzigerstrasse 110	
	Please look closely for house number "110"!	

No. 252, Oct. 27th, 1880

SATURDAY, THE 15TH OR 16TH OCT. we arrived in Berlin by means of the marvellous steam. At 9 p.m. we had left Hamburg, at 6 a.m. we arrived in Berlin at our house that we built ourselves; a beautiful house although only of boards. To wipe the floor of our house was nearly impossible because of all the people. Although they were thrown out by our masters, others quickly took their place. Between some trees we have a house. Nearby is a music house, a cause for astonishment. A lot of people wish to see our house, but it is impossible to be seen by all of

the Hall of Brethren next evening. Abraham's and his people's eyes got shiny when they were informed about this. I would like to give a more detailed description of this missionary evening but there should not be taken up too much space in this newsletter, but there will be more about this in the *Herrenhut*. That evening the Eskimos did not wear their seal fur but their white communion dress, they were happy about the suitable and rich meal which they consumed modestly in this close circle – their moving faces after singing in German and they were preached the word by Dr. Kern in their tongue, – the moment when the whole com-

them. Only a few have seen it, our masters even did not know whether we should ask someone in. When the teachers came they went in for the first time, but not immediately, because it was impossible due to all those people. Our enclosure was often broken by the throng. One day a great gentleman from Berlin came to see us and had many gentlemen with him. They all came into our enclosure to see the kayak but immediately everything was filled with people and it was impossible to move anymore. Both our masters Schoepf and Jacobsen shouted with big voices and

munity went down on their knees with them, and a heartfelt prayer closing with the Lord's prayer in Eskimo-language rose to the Lord who also followed his foolish lambs in this place, – the joy in their faces when they heard German choral singing and the sounds of the trumpets of the Kirdorfer brass band – those

are all pictures that will be unforgotten for all those who witnessed this evening. For a moment the sorrow about the consequences disappeared – at least that is what I have thought – that the hasty decision of Abraham and Tobias needs special help from the Lord; here the thanks for the Lord prevailed, to have

some of the higher-ranking soldiers left but most of them had no ears. Since our two masters did not achieve anything, they came to me and sent me to drive them out. So I did what I could. Taking my whip and the Greenland seal harpoon, I made myself terrible. One of the gentlemen was like a crier. Others quickly shook hands with me when I chased them out. Others went and jumped over the fence because there were so many. Several thanked me for doing this and our masters also thanked me very much. Ulrike had also locked our house from the inside and plugged up

souls among us who He gave the work of our brethren, weak children, but still children of the One Lord, who paid for them with His blood.

The impression of them should remain the same, when they visit us about the end of March in the community of Herrnhut – that is

what was promised them and us – after a long travel to Frankfurt A.M., Paris, Vienna and St. Petersburg via Dresden. We grew very fond of them. […]

BR. V. DEWITZ

the entrance so that nobody would go in, and those who wanted to look in through the windows were pushed away with a piece of wood.

✻

THE 11TH NOV. Few people. We got no money, because they were too few.

✻

THE 11TH NOV. I saw Elsner, who (from Bremen) came to see us. He came with (Emperor) Wilhelm's teacher (court

BREMEN, JANUARY 18TH , 1881

DEAR BROTHER REICHEL!

Today, I have to deliver to you a report that deeply moves me and all others, and tell you that *all* the Eskimos in Paris have been called home by the Lord. I believe that, with my last lines to you, which I noted on the envelope of the letter, I told you that the second child of Abraham and Ulrika had passed away. That news had also reached me through Mr. Hagenbeck. A short while later (two or three days after) Mr. H. told me in response to my inquiry, and presumably in reaction to my wire

---

preacher Stöcker) and another one. They prayed because of us that we don't turn from the Lord and may not get lost. Also some religious women came to our hut and sang and led the prayers very greatly. Yes indeed, we have the believers here in Germany as our brothers and sisters, they even called us brothers and sisters, even cried in front of us that we might not get lost through the Satan, they even knelt down in front of us reverentially, by greeting they often strengthen us greatly; and thought at the same time to tell our souls something strengthening by doing so.

telegram, "that I would not be admitted to the Eskimos suffering from smallpox in Paris."

Thus it became easier for me to decide to abstain from the trip to Paris for the time being until he Lord would smooth the path of a journey which has been so full of serious obstacles until now; but this does not mean at all that I had given up the journey altogether.

But then, tonight, we were overwhelmed by the sad news of their departure from life, which has also affected Mr. Hagenbeck very profoundly. The news from Paris seems to be based on a wire telegram, and there are no further details. Mr. Hagenbeck adds the follow-

ESDRAIGE (AUSTRIA) I am writing in Prague here far away, in Austria, in the country of Catholics, in a big city. We are here for two weeks, inside a big long house. To go out is impossible, so that we may not be caught by the Catholics. Yes indeed, we are highly regarded and have a house in the big house. It also has a seal, coming from Holland for us to eat, but it only is allowed to be stabbed with the seal harpoon. But until now I still have seen few believers, those, which are not from us. They sang with little voice because of shyness of the Catholics. We only

ing: "My managers will stay in Paris for another 14 days, and on their return trip will come to see you."

It is a great consolation in this very sad affair that the Eskimos were so thoroughly prepared for their passing, yes, were positioned for it. They brought no shame upon the Lord or the Mission, but wherever they went and even without words – because they were not understood – they were a testimony to the fact that the belief in the redeeming suffering of the Saviour, the belief in which they lived, provides a new heart and a new essence. They were free of the concerns of this earth except for the *sin-*

alone with little voice can we sing and pray here to get help from the Lord, so that nothing happens to us through the Catholics, because they are permanently asking if we are believers, so we are unable to deny and testify it constantly and only expect that they will do us harm. Yes indeed, because it is frightening here, so that we feel our being helped greatly. One day in the afternoon at 4 o'clock countless soldiers came; the big ways were totally filled. They carried fire as well as lanterns supplied with a handle; the horses had fire as well. But

gle wish: to see their relatives once again, but even in this they surrendered to the will of the Lord.

Brother Elsner

[Source: Moravian Archives at Herrnhut, Germany, R 19 Bf 16 b]

UAC MINUTES, JANUARY 22ND, 1881

In a letter of the 13th of January Br. Elsner writes in Bremen that he eventually gave up to travel to Paris to visit the Eskimos, who fell ill with smallpox, and bring them religious consolation, because in all probability he would not

Frankfurter Nachrichten

The Eskimos in the 'Zoologischer Garten'

☞ **December 3, 1880.** In the night from Nov. 30th to Dec. 1st, our city received a rare as well as interesting increase in population, namely two Eskimo families, eight heads altogether. The high ladies and gentlemen, or rather the ladies and gentlemen coming from high up north arrived just in time to be included in the census. Mr. Carl Hagenbeck from Hamburg, the one who earlier had introduced us to the children of the south, the Nubians, has also brought us these guests from the populated areas furthest up north. And children they are, these as well as those; because even if so-called culture has already had a pretty strong effect on them, for us there still remain enough interesting and natural things about them to be observed and maybe also admired.

As already known, we distinguish two tribes among these inhabitants of northern polar countries, who are quite different in their peculiarities: namely, the Greenlandic people, and those tribes who live at the coastlines of Labrador, meaning the American mainland. Our guests belong to the latter category; strictly speaking, they are under the head sovereignty of England. But England does not seem to care much for these "Her Majesty's subjects," at least there are no English officials in that region, so that these children of nature, still highly naïve in spite of efforts at civilization, are completely given into the hands of the Hudson Bay Company, respectively the Herrnhut Colony. Looking at the personal messages of Mr. J. A. Jacobsen, one could almost doubt if this is to their advantage. This man, who had been sent out on the instruction of Hagenbeck to go to the Eskimos in their home country and to induce them for their "art-journey" to the European mainland, cannot tell enough about how they live in dependence from the ones named above. Not only can the Eskimos obtain the things they need only through their mediation, the Eskimos are also personally dependent on them in such a way that nobody of them would, for example, try to even temporarily leave the country without their permission. But the Danish government in Greenland as well as the Herrnhuters in Labrador have their own pretty important reasons for keeping their subjects locked away, if possible from the whole outer world. They especially and firmly oppose a visit of them to Europe, for they well have to fear that these could on the occasion get to know some unpleasant things about the real value of the hunting products they bartered away in exchange, as well as about the real price of the materials they received.

After long wanderings between the west coast of Greenland, Cumberland, and Labrador, Mr. Jacobsen finally managed to find only two Eskimo families who, in spite of all, felt independent enough to take part in the journey to Europe. Since this journey was really tempting to all of them, and had it been possible, all the Eskimos living in Labrador, who are only about 2000 heads, would have liked to move to Europe in corpore. There are stories that were told by three fellow Inuit [from Greenland], the first to go to Europe three years ago, who have since related their travelling experiences and how they brought home quite considerable amounts of money. These stories have stirred the wish in the whole population to become rich in the same easy and pleasant way. Even so, Mr. Jacobsen could consider himself a happy man even to have won these two families for his undertakings, and after they had shown themselves in Berlin and

Prague they arrived here, as said above, late in the evening on the last day of November.

In the 'Zoologischer Garten' people had already set up two earth huts for them on the right and left side of the music pavilion. These huts are, even if not built by the Eskimos themselves, yet created in accordance with a model of the dwellings in their home country. The so-called wild Eskimos, i.e. the ones that could preserve their freedom to a certain extent and kept themselves independent from the missionaries, live in tents during the summer, but in earth huts in the winter, which are similar to those we can see built in the 'Zoologischer Garten'. They are dug into the earth as a shelter from the cold and consist of a wooden shed which is covered with piled up earth, here grass, on the outside. The real ice huts are only built by those who live that far up north that they cannot find any earth or driftwood. A tunnel, several yards long, and which always faces south, leads to the door of these huts. The inside, as far as we can see it here in the 'Zoologischer Garten', is neatly covered with boards, but, as Mr. Jacobsen asserts, the huts in Labrador also enjoy this luxury. There are even signs on the doors and door locks to the small huts, approximately 15 to 20 feet wide; the branches of the Herrnhuters cause this and have made these and many other luxury articles indispensable for the originally undemanding inhabitants. The only things that do not seem to be influenced by European culture are the semi-transparent windows made of seal intestines, one of which is at the roof of each of the huts. The shared sleeping place is opposite the entry, about half a metre above the ground. However, it is richly provided with furs but here again mattresses looking very civilized remind us of European cultural life.

The Christian Eskimo family dwells in the left hut, west of the music pavilion. They come from the Colony Nakkwak, which is quite far up north and consists of a family head, Abraham, his wife Ulrike, and their two daughters Sara and Marie, as well as their companion Tobias. Abraham is 35 years old; he is the most intelligent of all of them, even if not at all the most beautiful or, to be more precise, the least ugly one of the group. At the same time he takes the task of an interpreter, is able to read and write, is also said to be musical and to try his hand at drawings, but with moving into the new dwelling and the unpacking of all his possessions, the Northern whiz did not yet have the time and was not yet at leisure to show himself in all his variety. His wife Ulrike, even if not really a Venus, is but of reasonable looks, she is 24 years old and has the two chubby-cheeked children named earlier, the oldest of whom is 3? years and the youngest not even one year old. Tobias, the companion, is at the happy age of 21 years, and being neither worried about military service nor, probably, by any other awkwardness connected with culture totally unknown to him, he gives the impression of a perpetually smiling full-moon-face shining from fish oil. We probably do not need to go into details about the looks of all of the ladies and gentlemen here, because these looks are already known too well through pictures and texts, and the Eskimos present here do in general live up to the expectations we are used to have of them. All of them have a short, stocky physique and, even if they are not of the same dwarfish size as their namesakes from Greenland, they still do rarely reach the medium size. Because their clothes made of seal-furs they seem to be even stockier and plumper than they really are. In addition, when we imagine the head, growing quite thick, long and straggly black hair, the leathery yellow complexion, the slanted, deep-set eyes and the big mouth we will get a picture bringing together ugliness, good nature, and comic aspects in the most pleasant way. The latter, the comic aspects, especially, become obvious with the women because of their peculiar clothing. Besides the obligatory seal-boots and trousers they wear a tail-like upper dress, the appendage of which dangles after them like a beaver tail. A big hood completes this promenading dress, which is not subject to any Paris fashion, and Mrs. Ulrike, married to Abraham, simply uses the hood, now also back in fashion among our women, to put her child Marie in. These women's seal-tails appear even funnier when it is cold and a second, third, even fourth layer of them is put on. One is actually quite mistaken to believe that the Eskimos were tough and to a high degree insensitive to cold. Just the opposite is the case, and they can only protect themselves against the harsh effects the cold has on them with the help of their extremely warm clothing, and experience shows that we as Europeans can stand the harshness of the Nordic climate much more easily than the native people. Thus yesterday morning, with the temperature still some degrees over zero, we could see the women running around with two tail-coats, one on top of the other. By the way, this whole "national costume" does, at least in the family converted to Christianity, disappear very quickly, and the women at the mission are even already ashamed of it and particularly like to follow European fashion and to wear wool skirts. Only with much trouble could the members of Abraham's family be persuaded to return to their forefathers' custom during their stay in Europe. But this did not happen unconditionally either, because we can see European vests and shirts peeking out from under the seal furs the men wear, while four-year-old Sara protects her head with a crocheted wool hood, although even she already possesses beaver tail and hood. By the way, the dresses made from seal furs, in spite of all awkwardness in form, do not lack a certain elegance, because the makers knew how to get good variations into them with the combination of different kinds of fur.

The second one of the huts, east of the music pavilion accommodates the second family, not yet converted to Christianity; it consists of the Tigganick, about 40-year-old, his wife Paieng, probably ten years older, and their 15-year-old daughter Noggasack. The family is more interesting than the one named first, in so far as culture has not smudged too much of their naturalness. In their home country, they are happy to live together with three other families, cut off from the whole world, without any knowledge of "authorities" and everything connected with that. The survival instinct controls their whole life, they do not know any other task than to supply their stomach with fat and their lamp with fish oil, a task which, under the prevailing circumstances, certainly seems big enough to fill a whole human life. Besides that, Tigganick also acts as a magician, in which he is faithfully supported by his better half. Madam Paieng is the complete model of female ugliness, however, she is said to be a dame with considerable natural wit, in contrast to Miss Noggasack, her daughter, who is said to be of great stupidity. Besides, these so-called wild Eskimos, too, have very quickly got used to the blessings of culture, at least with regard to food, because even if in the first days of their stay in Europe they demanded and received their national drink, fish-liver oil, they do not long for it anymore and are happy with fish and meat alone.

The Eskimos do of course have their entire household and fishing gear with them; furthermore they also brought a pack of the famous, half-wild dogs with them, which they use to drag their sleds. They are quite fabulous, wolf-like, strong animals which, according to the statements of their leaders, are dumb, disobedient, and voracious, so that their masters can only manage to keep them in order with the help of the colossal whip. The grey animals belong to the Greenlandic race, while the black ones live in Labrador. In the morning of the day before yesterday, when we had the possibility to observe the strangers, they could not yet show us their facilities in driving the dog-sled, nor their boating with their famous kayaks, but they will well make up for this during the next days. Besides, Mr. Hagenbeck has also brought a large collection of Greenlandic antiquities and equipment of the native people, an exhibition of which was put up yesterday.

they have also made beautiful voice (music), most delightful to hear, with the trumpets.

✡

NOV. 27TH Have purchased a seal (Netsek) in Prague in a pond, while there were enormously many people, yes indeed countless. When I harpooned it with the seal harpoon, everybody clapped their hands greatly like the Eider ducks. When I had it ready, the voicemakers sang greatly with violins, drums, trumpets, and flutes. Yes indeed, to talk

have been allowed to visit them because of the infection or if they had allowed it he would have been kept back as long as it was proved that no infection had occurred [...]

UAC MINUTES, JANUARY 23RD, 1881

Hebron, August 16th 1880. As early as August 5th the letters by *Cordelia* & *Harmony* arrived – The death of the little Albert Haugk, due to the scalds when he fell into hot water, was a very hard experience for the brothers and

to each other was impossible because of the many voices.

From Prague, we left for Frankfurt, where it has many people. There we had two houses in the open in an enclosure. In our whole village grove, we were guarded day and night by soldiers, which took turns. It has many Jews there; the Catholics are very greatly despised there. But there we very often paddled kayak even on a pond.

From there, we went away again in a sleigh with wheels and horses in the night, all of us, to Darmstadt.

sisters. Incidentally, the death was peaceful in the outer and inner way. When on the 10th of August Mr. Jakobsen from Hamburg arrived in a schooner, travelling on behalf of the menagerie owner Hagenbeck and among other things looking for Eskimos for exhibitions in European cities, the brothers and sisters explained to him that they neither could nor wanted to help him with that. He could not share the objections, and despite their resistance the plans almost worked out, because a family would have already agreed if Mr. Jakobsen had not only been interested in eight to ten persons. Since the brothers and sisters

Paingo
(1830?–1880)

Terrianiak
(1840?–1881)

Noggasak
(1856?–1880)

In Darmstadt, we have had a beautiful house in a beautiful big round house, which is a playground for ice-skating on wheels. There we often sleighed round and round inside the house, all of us sitting on it. There one of us, Terrianiak's daughter, Nochasak, stopped living very fast and suffered terribly greatly. After her, in another country, in Krefeld, her mother also died, greatly suffering as well. After her, also little Sara stopped living in peace with a great rash and swellings, because she was swollen all over. After two days of being sick, she died in Krefeld.

wanted to know how they should act in those situations, [...] gave his full approval to their behaviour.

The contribution to the mission is £ 2 12 4. G. Kretschmer/W. Haugk, Ad. Hlawatschek

UAC MINUTES, FEBRUARY 24TH, 1881

C. G. KRETSCHMER. HEBRON, AUGUST 20TH, 1880.

In the burning of the boathouses and the destruction of the machine Kretschmer sees God's chastisement for the acquisition of a use-

While she was still alive, she was brought to hospital, where I went with her. She still had her mind, while I was there. She still prayed the song: "Ich bin ein kleines Kindelein" ("I am a child so small"). When I wanted to leave, she sent her greetings to her mother and little sister. When I left her, she slept; from then on, she did not wake up anymore. For this we both had reason to be thankful. While she was still alive, we went away to Paris and travelled the whole day and the whole night through.

less, expensive luxury item. Afterwards he reports in detail that eventually, Abraham and his family let themselves be won over by Mr. Jakobsen, and he insists that this happened with their knowledge but against their will. In spite of their most urgent pleading Abraham could not be moved against his decision, and therefore they were free of all responsibilities for the consequences.

Zeitschrift für Ethnologie
Volume 12, 1880

Eskimos at the Berlin Zoo

by Dr. Rudolf Virchow

[The following excerpts are translations of an article in which Dr. Rudolf Virchow (1821-1902), a renowned physician of Berlin, describes his experiences with the Inuit visitors. He examined them during their stay in the zoological garden in Berlin and analyzed various features concerning their outward appearance and culture. These were (ab)used to get a somewhat "scientific approach" to their heritage and their cultural status, meaning that they "get into one line with the lowest races of other parts of the world" (p. 268).

The examinations included:

Detailed physical analysis and measurements, e.g. face and body proportions, shape of the eyes, skin color, etc.
Education
Aspects of perception, e.g. how Inuit see and describe colors
Linguistic features
Use of tools, etc.

The article was published in Zeitschrift für Ethnologie *[Journal of Ethnology], Vol. 12. Berlin: Verlag von Paul Parey, 1880. pp. 253-274.]*

Although coming from the same area in Labrador, which is situated on almost the same latitude as the southern tip of Greenland, the Eskimos we are dealing with can be said to be comprised of two groups or families. They belong to coherent groups who differ not only in their religion but show several differences in their outer appearance as well.

One group, the family of Abraham, consisting of the man, the woman Ulrike and two small children – along with the unmarried Tobias, come from the mission of Hebron.... the missionaries were successful in supporting the education of these people to such an extent that they developed their intelligence to quite a degree and are capable of writing easily, of drawing, and of practicing several skills of a civilized life.... The other family, consisting of the man Tiggianiak, his wife Paieng, and his daughter Noggasak, however, are completely heathenish and, indeed, possess features that are eminently fit for learning about the primitive state of this people. Mr. Jacobson hired this family in Nakkwak, a station of the Hudson Bay Company at a fjord north of Hebron.

* * *

The hair of our people from Labrador matches that of the people from Greenland in every respect. The color of the hair is black without exception. Already the small children have very dark hair, only the eyebrows are rather brownish. The adult men's hair is relatively long so that it covers the neck and even the shoulders of the heathens. It is very thick, shiny black, like ebony, similar to the manes of horses, by no means curly or wavy but very straight. The women's hair has the same quality, only they have it comparatively short and thus it rather gives the impression of a certain sparseness. Mrs. Ulrike has hers simply parted and braided. In contrast, the pagan woman and her daughter have a knot at the neck and at every temple, the knots at the temples are

trimmed with long pendants which are plaited of reindeer hair and richly decorated with colourful (European) pearls. The eyebrows of most of them are thick, only Mrs. Ulrike's are thinner. Even the men hardly ever have sideburns, whereas moustache and goatee are thicker, only that the latter is restricted to the chin. A bit of a moustache can also be found on Mrs. Ulrike. The rest of the body, as far as I had a look at it, chest, forearm, lower leg, are almost completely hairless.

* * *

It is known, and here I want to oppose especially the purists in this field, that if we ask our common people, e.g. rural peasants, we also observe that some of them cannot distinguish these colors precisely and that they set up similar combinations, as they occur here, through nuancing the color blue and thus saying "black-blue" or "dark-blue" or "red-blue." Altogether, the Eskimos that we interrogated individually exhibited such strong homogeneity in their answers that it cannot be disputed on linguistic congruence. They are obviously predisposed in this direction and prove to be not of a lower but of a relatively higher race, not in the sense believed by many for a long time, that the retina only develops with the culture.

One also has to judge their intelligence in a similar way, I think. Nothing has ever more forcefully strengthened the impression that the Eskimos are of a lower race than their clumsiness in using numbers.... Indeed, one can imagine that the need to count is very small in a population whose members live so far apart and have few possessions and do not domesticate animals, except dogs. But yet, that large number of dogs that they need to drive their sleighs indicates that they must have some sort of substitute for counting with words. In any case, the Christianized people prove that their brains, indeed, are able to develop, as is seen in artistic achievements, even of the wild Eskimos, in numerous tests. Especially Abraham, who seems to have enjoyed a complete education, proves to be one of the most educated and smartest individuals one can see, according to my examinations.

* * *

You will probably be interested in learning something about the fit that I observed with Mrs. Bairngo the other day. You have now seen how shy the daughter is; she looks like a wild animal that has been captured. The mother does not have this squeamish nature, but she is extremely suspicious so that one realizes, with every step she takes in any place she is not familiar with, how much the new environment causes grave concern within her. It was very hard to take her measurements, which was rather easy with the others. I started with the simplest, and thus tried to convince her little by little that it was nothing harmful; but every new act caused her concern again, and when it was time to measure her body she began to shake alarmingly.

While I was spreading her arms horizontally, because I wanted to take her fathom length, which seems to have never occurred in her entire life, she suddenly had the fit: she slipped underneath my arm and started "carrying on all over" the room with such a fury and in such a way as I have never seen before, although I encountered the most extraordinary fits of anger and cramps, be it simulated or real, as a long-term doctor in a prison. At first, I expected it to turn into a hysterical catatonic fit. But soon it became clear that absolutely no physical cramp, nothing somatic, arose. It rather went on as a psychic cramp, comparable to what people perform in a state of highest rage. In such a state, people may rush around in the room, smash everything they can grab, and do the strangest things, about which they remember nothing afterwards. This case was similar. She jumped through the room on both legs and in a slightly bent position "worked" chairs and tables and threw them in all directions. But while she was romping through the room, she never even tried to slip out the door or to attack one of the persons present. She jumped from one corner into the other and was screaming with a crying voice, her ugly face looked dark red, her eyes were glowing, and there was a bit of foam at her mouth; to sum it up: it was a highly disgusting sight.

At the same time it was highly surprising to see the man and the daughter sitting on their chairs all the time and not showing the slightest bit of excitement or attempt to help. The attack lasted about eight to ten minutes; then all of a sudden she stood still, laid her head on the table, stayed in that position for a few minutes, then raised herself again and said in her own language: "Now I'm good again." Of course, she was still shaking and I

considered it advisable not to make a new attempt to measure her. I had the impression that this "psychic cramp" must be exactly the same form of appearance that the shamans perform in their dances.

As everybody knows, getting used to excessive personal excitement (that mainly occurs in shamanism) is mostly kept alive through a long tradition in the north-eastern part of Asia. However, there are also visible traces of this in Greenland where the shamans are called Angekoks.

* * *

I want to restrict myself to these comments, yet I beg your indulgence to briefly reject a strong attack that was published in the *Magdeburger Zeitung* recently (no. 493 of October 21st).

On the one hand, this article is aimed at the whole way of developing ideas about foreign races. On the other hand, it argues against the use of zoological gardens for the exposition of human beings. Since it is a newspaper which acts as the organ of this attack, and since we are living in a time when all kinds of things happen that seem to be impossible, it seems imperative to me to oppose categorically this first attack of a bewildered feature writer.

In an article entitled "Die Eskimos im Zoologischen Garten zu Berlin" ["The Eskimos in the zoological garden in Berlin"] the author does not only oppose the exhibition of human beings, but he also declares explicitly that at second thought it can be expected that one would move away from showing human beings in zoological gardens. I will quote the ending briefly: "We are totally prepared to have our opinion smiled at and ridiculed as sentimental by some. Nevertheless, we have wanted to express it here. If these "interesting" human specimens need to be exhibited at all, a sense of "racial ethics" should prevent us from displaying our equals in zoos. It should be easy to identify appropriate localities elsewhere."

The argumentation, which is based mainly on this consideration, starts with the fact – and this is what I actually want to consider – that there is no scientific interest, and that for the majority of the people there exists nothing but sheer curiosity. The feature writer indulges himself occasionally, saying: "However, it is very interesting" – as if that were a reproach. In this respect it seems that this gentleman does not realize that the "interest" itself can be diverse. Some things are only interesting as curiosities, however, those things we are exploring on behalf of science, like the progressing exploration of nature and human beings, are mainly brought home to us because they are interesting. Indeed, these theories about human beings are interesting for everybody who wants to be informed about our position within nature and our evolution.

Those who cannot understand that the most important and magnificent questions that mankind can ask are driven by our curiosity about ourselves seem least qualified to write features. An editorial staff should at least think twice before including such comments in its papers.

That is what I wanted to ensure. Furthermore, I testify that a positive scientific interest of the highest rank is connected with this attitude. Therefore, I do not want to miss the chance to thank Mr. Hagenbeck in public and to advise him that he should not let himself be kept from continuing the exhibitions in the manner he has done before – as he has done it up until now with the greatest benefit for anthropological science.

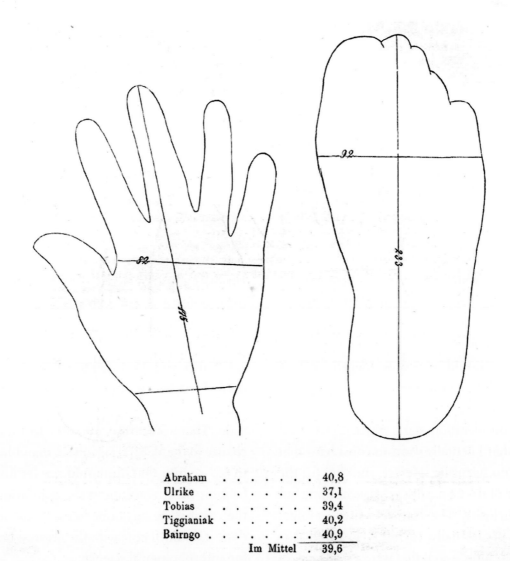

Abraham	. . . .	40,8
Ulrike	. . . .	37,1
Tobias	. . . .	39,4
Tiggianiak	. . . .	40,2
Bairngo	. . . .	40,9
	Im Mittel .	39,6

(On January 8, 1881, five days before his own death, Abraham wrote once again to his friend and teacher Br. Elsner, this time from Paris. This letter was published in Missionsblatt der Brüdergemeinde in March 1881.)

My dear teacher Elsner!

I write to you in a very despondent mood and I am even very distressed, due to my relatives; because our child, who I loved so much, is also not living anymore, she had died of the evil smallpox; four days after the outbreak of her sickness she passed away. My wife and I will be very soon reminded through the death of the child that we also have to die. She died in Krefeld, although she had many doctors. Those indeed could not do anything; we especially wanted to have Jesus as our doctor, who died for us. My dear teacher Elsner! We kneel down in front of him all days, bent because of our presence here and ask him that he will forgive our aberration; we also do not doubt that the Lord will hear us. All day we cry mutually, that our sins will be taken away by Jesus Christ. Even Terrianiak, who is now alone, when I say to him that he should convert, desires to become a property of Jesus, sincerely, as it seems. He constantly takes part in our prayers until this day, such as my child Maria. But even her life is doubtful, because her face is very swollen, also Tobias is sick, although many doctors come they cannot help. I remember very well that only one can help when our death time comes, yes indeed. He is everywhere where we too are. I really wish I could tell my relatives, who are over there, how friendly God is; indeed, my wife also sheds easily tears because of our sins. Our superior does buy a lot of medicine, no doubt, but all this still does not help; but I trust in God that He will answer my prayers and will collect all my tears every day. I do not long for earthly possessions but this is what I long for: to see my relatives again, who are over there, to talk to them of the name of God as long as I live. I hadn't grasped this before, now I understand. I shed my tears fast, but the words uttered by Himself console us very much again and again.

My dear teacher Elsner, pray for us to the Lord that the evil sickness will stop if it is His will; but God's will be fulfilled. I am a poor man who's dust.

Also in Paris it is cold, in fact very cold; but our superior is very kind to all of us now. I'll write again soon. I send you my regards, and my wife sends hers as well to everyone in the unity of Bremen.

I am Abraham, Ulrika's husband

If you write to the great teachers, tell them that we send our greetings to them.

The Lord be with you all! Amen.

Appendix A: Abraham's Diary and Inuit Autobiography

In our own translation (into English) of Kretschmer's translation (from Inuktitut into German) of Abraham's diary, we tried to keep the awkward and grammatically flawed style of Kretschmer's text. We do not know whether Kretschmer's "incompetent" style is the result of a hasty translation, or a verbatim rendering of an Inuktitut syntax, which might sound awkward in German, or whether it may also be the result of Kretschmer's partial loss of his mother tongue after years of living in a linguistic diaspora.

The very first entry of Abraham's diary is expressive of the Inuk's severe culture shock, caused by the constant and high level of noise and the unfamiliar experience of crowds of people. Again and again, Abraham expresses his dismay at the unruly throngs pressing into their enclosure and even into the houses they had in the zoos where they were exhibited. In one case, neither their "guardian," Jacobsen, nor the military officers present could move the crowds to leave the compound, until finally they asked Abraham to scare off the visitors. Abraham accomplished this task with the help of a Greenland seal harpoon, a dog whip and, apparently, his "savage" looks: "Taking my whip and the Greenland seal harpoon I made myself terrible."

The Inuit suffered from health problems incurred by the wet cold and psychologically intensified by their isolation. Other entries document some of the intense emotional stress inflicted upon the Inuit by their "master," on whose actions they depended so precariously. For November 7th, 1880, Abraham reports that Captain Jacobsen beat Tobias with a dog whip for disobedience, and that afterwards the abused "was very sick." In hindsight, Jacobsen must have felt remorse or have feared a scandal. Abraham mentions that the Captain asked him not to report this incident to the Moravians, and that Jacobsen bought silk ribbons for the women. Obviously, Abraham was aware that his literacy offered a potential safeguard against further abuse, because he mentions his resolution to write to the Moravians

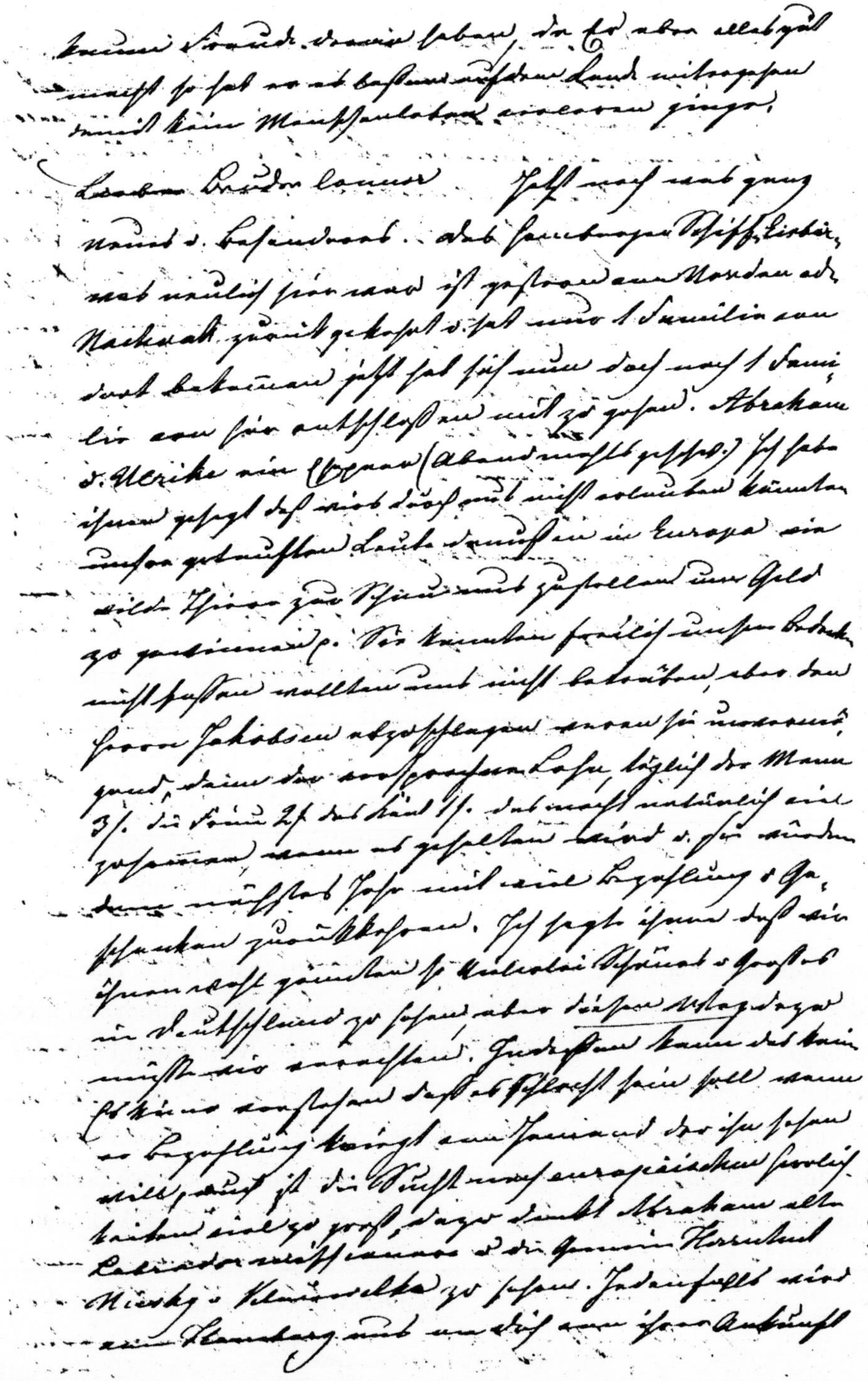

A page from the German transcription of Abraham's diary.

in England, should Jacobsen repeat such behaviour.

The Inuit travellers fervently hoped for, and at the same time feared, the return voyage across a North Atlantic, which had made them so seasick before. Their fears are reflected in Abraham's brief entry about the news of ships having sunk in the North Sea. He and his Moravian family had also been instilled with a paranoid fear of members of other denominations, which kept them from going out in Prague, "so that we may not be caught by Catholics" (November 11th). The Hussites were pre-reformation religious dissenters, to whom the Moravian Brethren traced their tradition. They had been ruthlessly persecuted and mercilessly killed by the Catholic Church in the 15th century. This historical trauma likely caused deeply felt fears of Catholicism, which the Moravian teachers seem to have passed on to Abraham. In Frankfurt am Main, November 27th, he notes: "There are many Jews here, the Catholics are very greatly despised there." Again, Abraham took special note of Catholics, but there are no other comments about Jews, and from the text we cannot learn whether Abraham saw them as threatening, whether he had learned to share widespread Christian anti-Judaism, or why else he should feel their presence needed special mention.

For the Christian Inuit, there were contacts with, and encouraging visits by, members of the "Herrnhuter Brüdergemeinde," as the Moravian Brethren are called in German. The highlights of their stay, we may gather from Abraham's diary, were visits to an elaborate Moravian church service with much singing, praying, and music. A tour of a Berlin wax museum exposed the visitors to an inverted and twisted "colonial gaze," since the museum's ethnographic show exhibited life-like figures of "Nubians, Africans ..., and Chinese and Indians and Americans and Californians, yes indeed, the inhabitants of the earth," as Abraham put it in his October 27th entry. Besides, he wrote enthusiastically about a military parade in Prague, and he was obviously proud of their various rides by train, tram, and sleigh, including a steam engine "faster than flying ones" in a first class carriage "which great gentlemen usually use" (November 10th).

Occasionally, Abraham's text mentions the work they were paid for: the ethnographic demonstrations, showing how they displayed their arts and crafts, how they paddled their kayaks on a pond that was covered with ice they had to break first, or how they harpooned a live seal brought from Holland, upon which the audience "clapped their hands greatly like the Eider ducks" (November 27th). In addition, Abraham had to show off his "civilized" accomplishments like playing the violin, drawing sketches, or writing his name. He also recorded when their intake from visitors was very low: "Sometimes we are given some money, sometimes 2 pence, sometimes 1 mark, sometimes 50" (November 10th).

Their monotonous and obviously inadequate diet of hardtack, herring or cod, coffee, and beer was occasionally broken by treats like fresh fruit given them by sympathetic spectators. Whenever Brethren from their church came for brief visits, Abraham seems to have been filled with genuine delight, and he entertained high hopes of visiting the Moravian centre at Herrnhut. Gradually, however, Abraham's homesickness becomes ever more obvious in his writings. In his letters to his former teacher (missionary) Brother Elsner in Bremen, he pours out his heart in confessions that are both religious and secular. His letters also record his economic and intellectual motives for having agreed to the voyage: he

was in debt and hoped to earn enough to pay back his debts to the mission and to buy a net – and he was curious to see Europe. The letter tells Brother Elsner, how he repented his foolish decision to have agreed to this trip. He expresses his fervent longing to return to Labrador "to see my relatives again."

In his last letter, Abraham reports the death of his daughter Sara, and how he and Ulrike hope that the Lord would "forgive our aberration" (to have agreed to the trip against the Moravians' counsel). The last entry in the diary, which we had the greatest emotional difficulty in translating, reads:

From there we went away again in a sleigh with wheels and horses in the night, all of us, to Darmstadt.

In Darmstadt, we have had a beautiful house in a beautiful big round house, which is a playground for ice-skating on wheels. There we often sleighed round and round inside the house, all of us sitting on it. There one of us, Terrianiak's daughter, Nochasak, stopped living very fast and suffered greatly terribly. After her, in another country, in Krefeld, her mother also died, greatly suffering as well. After her, also little Sara stopped living in peace with a great rash and swellings, because she was swollen all over. After two days of being sick, she died in Krefeld.

While she was still alive, she was brought to hospital, where I went with her. She still had her mind, while I was there. She still prayed the song: *Ich bin ein kleines Kindelein* (I am a child so small). When I wanted to leave, she sent her greetings to her mother and little sister. When I left her, she slept; from then on, she did not wake up anymore. For this we both had reason to be thankful. While she was still alive, we went away to Paris and travelled the whole day and the whole night through (November 27th).

The diary as a whole is a deeply depressing document, since, despite brave protestations to the contrary, there is an increasing sense of doom. But while Abraham's diary and letters occasionally provide expressions of his delight at meeting his Brethren or enjoying sightseeing trips, the situation of Terrianiak, Noggasak, and Paingo must have been abysmal and unbearably bleak. Abraham reported in his first letter to Brother Elsner: "We are very grateful that they have a home for themselves. We don't like their habits, they both practise magic. I often ask them to convert, but it doesn't help." We also learn from Abraham's few comments in the diary, that as early as October 27th the Northerners "stopped being cheerful, because they are tired of the people." Later, on the train to Berlin, according to Abraham, Terrianiak "worked magic" but was "extremely distraught by his witchcraft and couldn't smile at anyone" (November 10th). In his first letter to Brother Elsner, Abraham reports that Paingo "is sick, very sick," but that they "reject taking any medicine, they hope to get well by magic." Upon their arrival in Paris, Terrianiak's entire family had been wiped out by smallpox. The shaman must have been completely broken in spirit. Abraham reported in his last letter:

Even Terrianiak, who is now alone, when I say to him that he should convert, desires to become a property of Jesus, sincerely, as it seems. He constantly takes part in our prayers until this day (January 8th).

Our empathy with the human suffering of these eight visitors to our country only 125 years ago was the primary motivational force for my students and myself to translate Abraham's diary, and to try to make it available to a non-German reading public in Canada, especially hoping that there might still be descendents of Terrianiak's and Abraham's extended families, who might be interested to read the diary. We were also motivated by the historical, geographic, and cultural contexts and legacies, which connect us to both the Inuit visitors and their missionaries and "masters." But for us as students of English language literature, there was and is also the scholarly interest in an old manuscript, and to do a translation not as an academic exercise, but "for real." There was a sense of being touched by history, as students went and discovered newspaper articles, or learned about *Völkerschauen*, Moravians in Labrador, or scientific racism in the late nineteenth century. Besides, Abraham's diary is not just an unusual historical document, but, to our knowledge, it is also the very first Inuit autobiographical text – a claim that may need some explanation.

Next to the oral tradition, autobiography is the most frequently used form of literary self-expression and self-definition by Aboriginal peoples in North America. Inuit writers and readers share a particularly rich, albeit comparatively recent autobiographical tradition. As in the case of Native American and Canadian First Nations writings, the earliest forms of Inuit literature are the results of literacy programs run by missionaries. Abraham's diary is no exception. Yet, it is different in several ways. While in the U.S. Native autobiography as a genre flourished in the nineteen twenties and thirties, in Canada it began after WWII and seems to have reached a peak in the nineteen seventies. This apparent time lag may be due to different developments in Native/non-Native relations and in different government strategies regarding Native cultures, as well as to the overall development of Canadian literature in general. It is most obvious in Inuit literary history. But within this context, Abraham's diary stands out as having been written almost a century before Inuit autobiographies began to be published in Canada on a more perceivable scale.

After the closure of the "Old North" in 1947 with the sinking of the *Nascopie* (P. Pitseolak 135), ethnographers and missionaries hastened to record the "old life," as told to them by survivors of the original hunting, fishing, and gathering ways. Thirty years later, in the seventies, a considerable number of "as-told-to's" were published, i.e., forms of autobiography based on collaboration with non-Native listeners, recorders, translators, editors, and publishers. The life story of *Nuligak* (i.e., Bob Cockney) as recorded by the missionary Maurice Methayer (1966), the life story of the woman artist Pitseolak (1971), as well as the life story of the photographer Peter Pitseolak (1975), both recorded and published by Dorothy Eber, are the most famous examples of this early form of Inuit autobiography. Soon followed "real" autobiographies, written by the authors themselves, such as Elizabeth Goudie's *Woman of Labrador* (1973), Anthony Apakark Thrasher's *Skid Row Eskimo* (1976) and Minnie Aodla Freeman's *Life Among the Quallunaat* (1978). All of them record, from each individual's perspective, the abrupt, traumatic change from traditional heritage ways to life in modern Canada. Minnie Freeman's book seems to confirm what can be said about Indigenous life histories in general, namely, that individuals endowed with a strong ethnic cultural identity and a sound knowledge of their traditional heritage seem to be empowered to more successfully avoid the dangers of being uprooted and ending up on skid row than those who were denied even an early traditional education, and who were therefore the more easily deracinated and (de)educated in the residential school system.

In more recent years, *Inuktitut* Magazine and the various Elders' conferences of the Inuit Cultural Institute have collected and published autobiographical pieces and life stories by Inuit elders still able to record the old way of life. In Labrador, *Them Days* Magazine specializes in local life histories. In 1980 Doris Saunders, founding editor of *Them Days*, published the earliest Inuit autobiographical text available in English, the account of her great-great-grandmother, Lydia Campbell, *Sketches of Labrador Life* (1893/94), which was republished in a beautiful edition with artwork by Labrador Inuit artists by Killik Press, St. John's Newfoundland, as recently as 2000.[1] Today,

---

[1] Doris Saunders has published a number of autobiographical accounts since, and my students and I had hoped she would also publish our translation of the Abraham diary, but after her first attempts were repeatedly thwarted by an uncooperative computer, she abandoned the project altogether, stating, "It's like it's cursed" (e-mail August 28th, 2002).

there are many conscious and concerted efforts by Inuit authors, editors and publishers, by historians, literary scholars and anthropologists to preserve as much oral knowledge as possible. In Nunavut, Inuit and non-Inuit community workers, educators, linguists, and anthropologists are collaborating to devise means of facilitating the transfer of traditional knowledge from the elders to their grandchildren,[2] since, as Basil Johnston once put it, the oral tradition is very precious and very brittle, being "only one generation removed from extinction" (Johnston 10).

In the light of such endeavours to preserve historical knowledge today, and when compared to all other forms of autobiographical writing, Abraham's diary falls through the generic grid. It is neither an as-told-to, nor, truly, a collaboratively co-authored one, nor do we possess material proof that the translation by Kretschmer is indeed based on an original text by the hand of Abraham Ulrikab. Still, we are certain it is as authentic as any autobiographical text, which is always a construction. Why, otherwise, would Brother Kretschmer have created it? Why would he have crossed out a passage on Terrianiak's "witchcraft," or why would he have written it in such garbled German? Given the almost naïve trust the Herrnhuters held for Hagenbeck and Jacobsen, two shrewd businessmen, it is inconceivable that one of the missionaries would have invented this life-story, which casts such doubts on Jacobsen's character. Besides, Abraham's diary is substantially corroborated by contextual evidence.

Unless the unlikely happens, and older autobiographical texts are (re)discovered, Abraham's diary is undoubtedly the oldest Inuit autobiography in existence, and a very unique one at that.

---

[2] In a joint presentation on "The Construction of a New Inuit Identity in Nunavut" at the conference on "First Nations of North America: Politics and Representation," at Middelburgh, Netherlands, 29th - 31st May 2002, Clara Aupalu, Jarich Oosten, and Cor Remie reported about an "interviewing" program in schools which required young Inuit students to go out and interview and record elders, thereby breaking down the children's shyness to approach elders, and the elders' traditional inhibitions to give advice without being asked, thus smoothing the generational transfer of knowledge by providing a new frame in which each generation has a socially acceptable role to play.

Appendix B:
German Contexts

ABRAHAM'S SHORT DIARY and two letters provide subjective and necessarily limited accounts of the journey but cannot convey an idea of the complicated processes involved in bringing over the Inuit group, nor of what happened before and after their visit. As further textual sources to consult there are a number of Moravian materials, contemporary newspaper accounts, Virchow's scholarly article, Captain Jacobsen's diary, and the memoirs of Carl Hagenbeck. These sources are not here presented in any detail. Our focus was to present the voice of Abraham. The following account, however, may help to contextualize historically and ideologically Abraham's tragic story.

The visit by the Labrador Inuit took place only a decade after the founding of the German national state, the *Kaiserreich*, in 1871, and the newly-founded German Empire was seeking to enter the international arena, flexing its muscle to become established as an imperialist colonial power, eager for its "place in the sun." In this ideological climate, there was an immense interest not only in foreign countries and their raw materials, their plants and animals, but also in "exotic" peoples and their cultures. *Völkerschauen*, which might be translated as "peoples exhibitions," provided ethnographic peep shows of cultures perceived by Europeans as "primitive" and altogether alien and inferior, but at the same time as curiously exciting and even desirable "Others." Only a decade later, from America, Buffalo Bill's Wild West Show would tour major European cities, but in the late 1870s in Germany, Carl Hagenbeck was the first to come up with the idea of satisfying the German "colonial gaze" by "importing" Indigenous peoples from overseas to exhibit them and have them observed, both as living objects of ethnographic research, and as exotic fetishes of voyeuristic desires. In 1877, Hagenbeck had presented to the public a group of Inuit from Greenland, whom Jacobsen had "delivered." In 1880 Hagenbeck tried to repeat the earlier success. He knew of the popular curiosity. In his memoirs, published in 1909, he praises his relationship with the Greenlanders, but he never mentions the economic flop and human catastrophe of this 1880 venture with Abraham and the others from Labrador. The account would not have fitted his self-celebratory success story.

Like Jacobsen, the would-be ethnologist, Hagenbeck also was keenly aware of the scientific interest. At the time, biologists, physicians, historians, anthropologists, linguists, and members of the fledgling *Völkerkunde* (peoples science, ethnography) were eager to weigh, measure, observe, and interview "primitives," and to assign them "their" definite place within a hierarchically structuring theory of human "races." Based on ethnocentric ideas about the genetic evolution of humans, their research invariably and automatically placed Europeans complacently at the top of the evolutionary scale. One of the most salient methods of asserting "racial" differences became measuring dimensions of the human body and expressing proportional relationships between body parts in "objective" mathematical equations or correlations, so-called anthropometry. Particularly widespread became the study of facial features and human skulls (phrenology, craniology). The interest in this empirical method (craniometry), or rather the general interest in phrenology, was

shared, for example, by Johan Wolfgang von Goethe (1749–1832), Germany's most prominent literary figure. His and his contemporaries' approach went back to neo-classical studies of antiques, especially classical Greek statues, as embodiments of perfect beauty and harmony, whose body proportions and profiles were seen as paradigmatic and ideal,[1] whereas deviations from that ideal were read as deficiencies not only physical but also mental and moral – there was a belief in phrenology, for example, that certain individuals had a *Diebsknochen* (thief's bone), i.e. a certain identifiable bone structure in the skull which indicated a propensity for stealing.

The later move in phrenology from lofty idealism to concrete discrimination, based on physical differences, must have been a gradual

---

[1] Examples of such scientific studies are found in the works of Adolph Zeising (1810–1876), who wrote several articles and books about the golden number (*goldener Schnitt*) in nature, especially in the proportions of the human body and facial features. He compared the dimensions and angles found in the profiles of classical statues with those of "Europeans," "Mongols," "Negroes," "Hottentots," "Americans," etc., and even "cretins," who all show up as "deviant" from the classic ideal. For the most substantial and diligently researched and documented account of Zeising's life and works, including a CD with archival materials, see: Roger Herz-Fischler, *Adolph Zeising: The Life and Work of a German Intellectual* (Ottawa: Mzinhigan Publishing, 2004).

and transient one, but after Darwin's pivotal biological study (*Origin of the Species*, 1859) and its utilization within the context of scientific racism, the intra-European and socially contained academic discussion gained prominence in ethnography and anthropology to classify all ethnic "others" into what was expected to be definable as distinct human races or even species. Ideologically, this development reflected and flanked the imperialist expansionism of the last part of the 19th century. The process of racially classifying human beings, widespread throughout 19th century Europe, culminated, as we all know, half a century later in the Nazi Third Reich, when, for the first time in recorded human history, political ideology assumed a god-like authority over the human right to life, basing its assumption of superior and absolute power on the constructed category of "race," which could supposedly be measured in terms of craniometrics, anthropometrics, and other "scientific methods," and thereupon decreeing that so-called "inferior races" were unfit, i.e. not "worthy" to live – and acted accordingly. At the time of Abraham's and the other Inuit's visit to Germany, the ideological consequences and later misuses of craniometry may not have

been imaginable, but the cold empiricist methodology of collecting human skulls and robbing Indigenous graves throughout the world, an enterprise Jacobsen was famous for, already seems to foreshadow the premeditating callousness, and merciless meticulousness of Nazi Germany's modernist mechanics for the systematic and industrialized destruction of fellow humans. But what were Jacobsen's, Hagenbeck's, and Virchow's motives at the time?

Quite obviously, Jacobsen's and Hagenbeck's incentives were primarily economic, and only professedly scientific. Jacobsen not only recruited Indigenous people for his employer's ethnographic shows, but he also collected, bought, or sometimes robbed, artefacts and human remains for museums in Europe. Carl Hagenbeck (1844–1913), like Abraham Ulrikab, had had a particularly unsuccessful economic year in 1879. The trade in zoo animals had been on the decline since the mid-seventies (Hagenbeck 80), and the shrewd businessman hoped to repeat the success of his earlier *Völkerschauen*, which he had begun in 1874 with a group of Sami people who had then accompanied a herd of reindeer imported from Northern Scandinavia.

But Hagenbeck's success as a businessman of *Völkerschauen* is only a minor component of his career. He is most famous for his campaign against the then prevalent cruel forms of training show animals by coercing them with hot irons and beating them into submission. By observing the natural behaviour of tigers, lions, bears, dogs, and other animals he trained, he managed to teach them by positive reinforcement without coercive measures, and he was the first circus showman to ride a chariot drawn by three seemingly peaceful lions. Later, he developed in Hagenbeck's Thierpark the first animal zoo in the world to keep animals not in barred cages but in open enclosures that recreated their natural habitat, a model gradually followed throughout the world. He also founded his own circus, practicing gentler methods of animal training. Obviously, there was also a gentler side to Hagenbeck's character.

The scholarly interest in the Inuit was expressed most prominently in the new field of anthropology. Dr. Rudolf Virchow (1821–1902) was then its foremost advocate in Germany. He had been the co-founder in 1869 of the German Anthropological Society and was the lifelong president of the Berlin Society for Anthropology, Ethnology, and Prehistory, established at the same time. But Virchow went down in history not for his works in *Völkerkunde* and archaeology – although he conducted archaeological digs and cooperated with Heinrich Schliemann, who discovered, unearthed, and plundered Troy – but rather for his achievements as a physician and social reformer: Rudolf Virchow pioneered the concepualization of pathological processes as starting in the cell, and he laid the foundation for modern medicine in Germany. Throughout his life he campaigned untiringly for the improvement of public health and social conditions in general. When the Prussian government sent him to Upper Silesia to investigate an outbreak of typhoid fever, he displeased his bosses because he blamed the government's inadequate social system for the epidemic. The unsuccessful German revolution of 1848 saw him on the barricades in Berlin, which temporarily cost him his professorship at the Charité, Berlin's most respected medical clinic. Later, as a member of the Berlin City Council, he founded hospitals and a nursing college, and he redesigned the city's sewage system. As a member of the *Fortschrittspartei* (Progressive Party) in the Reichstag, he was a bitter and personal opponent of Otto von Bismarck, who once challenged him to a duel, which Virchow declined. He obviously had backbone, but not the straightbacked and corseted type of the Prussian Junker. Virchow was the more enlightened of the two, and he must have had little patience for the vestiges of feudalism's traditional notions of a man's honour, because he later also declined the honour to be ennobled by the Kaiser and change his name to "*von Virchow.*" In other words, Virchow would be a German intellectual and reformer one tends to be in agreement with, and, were one a nationalist, one would like to be proud of. But when we look at his research in anthropometrics from our post–WW II perspective, the almost inevitable happens: the sunny picture becomes overcast by the stark shadow of our more recent past.

Virchow met the Labrador Inuit at least twice during their stay. Once he examined them and took their physical anthropometric data, and later he presented them to members of the Berlin Anthropological Society at their special meeting on November 7th 1880, the minutes of which were published shortly afterwards in his *Zeitschrift für Ethnologie*. It was at this special meeting that he informed members about the results of his previous examinations. In his report, Rudolf Virchow applauds the Moravians' "civilizing" success with Abraham and his family:

> The missionaries were successful in supporting the education of these people to such an extent that they developed their intelligence to quite a degree and are capable of writing easily, of drawing, and of practicing several skills of a civilized life (Virchow 253).

By contrast, he describes Terrianiak and his family as "completely heathenish" and as possessing "features that are eminently fit for learning about the primitive state of this people" (253). Finally, he does concede, however, that all Inuit seem capable of becoming educated:

> In any case, the Christianized people prove that their brains, indeed, are able to develop, as is seen in artistic achievements, even of the wild Eskimos. Especially Abraham, who seems to have enjoyed a complete education, proves to be one of the most educated and

smartest individuals one can see, according to my examinations (267).

Virchow proceeded to measure his "samples" and to record some of their language. Throughout, his objective was to racially classify them and find out whether they constituted a "race" in themselves or whether and how they were related to "Mongolians" in Asia or the Inuit of Greenland. Skin colour, hair texture, length of arms and legs, width of feet, growth of beard, and so on were all deemed of scholarly interest and were recorded with the same attention to minutiae as variations in clothing or equipment. The Inuits' "clumsiness in using numbers," he concluded, strengthens "the impression that the Eskimos are of a lower race" (267).

The most dramatic and haunting part of his report is a moment in which Paingo literally jumped out of the confines of scientific objectification:

> While I was spreading her arms horizontally because I wanted to take her fathom length, which seems to have never occurred in her entire life, she suddenly had a fit: she slipped underneath my arm and started "carrying on all over" the room with such a fury and in such a way as I have never seen before, although I encountered the most extraordinary fits of anger and cramps, be it simulated or real, as a long-term doctor in a prison. At first, I expected it to turn into a hysterical catatonic fit. But soon it became clear that absolutely no physical cramp, nothing somatic arose. It rather went on as a psychic cramp, comparable to what people perform in a state of highest rage. In such a state, people may rush around in the room, smash everything they can grab, and do the strangest things about which they remember nothing afterwards. This case was similar.… The attack lasted about eight to ten minutes… I had the impression that this "psychic cramp" must be exactly the same form of appearance that the shamans perform in their dances. As everybody knows, getting used to excessive personal excitement (that mainly occurs in shamanism) is mostly kept alive through a long tradition in the north-eastern part of Asia. However, there are also visible traces of this in

Greenland where the shamans are called Angekoks. (transl. from Virchow, 271)

Here Paingo refused a subaltern position in the hierarchical subject–object relationship of researcher and researched. She assumed agency and literally leapt out of her objectification, thereby resisting the violation of her human dignity and privacy. Dr. Virchow, on the other hand, clung to his role as the supposedly disinterested scholar and neutral observer. He scientifically categorized, and at the same time "othered," and pathologized, Paingo's behaviour alternatively as a "fit," or "a psychic cramp," or as an anthropologically interesting example/sample of a "shamanistic reaction." The ambivalence and insecurity of his diagnosis seems to indicate how eager he must have been to reclaim his privileged position of authority as the male, white expert – a patriarchal stance similar to Jean-Martin Charcot's detached handling of "hysteric" patients in the Salpêtrière hospital in Paris in the 1880s, or to Sigmund Freud's psychoanalysis of Otto Breuer's treatment of Anna O. in Vienna a few years later.

But Virchow's authority, the very nature of his anthropological gaze, came under attack not only from Paingo. In his presentation to the members of the *Berliner Gesellschaft für Völkerkunde*, Virchow defends his and Hagenbeck's scientific interests against an article in *Magdeburgische Zeitung* of October 21st 1880, which he quotes as having criticized the prevalent "way of developing ideas about foreign races" and "the use of zoological gardens for the exposition of human beings." The unidentified author, "J.K.," had made fun of ethnology's and zoology's tendency to indiscriminately find all minutae "interesting." Moreover, s/he had maintained that "a sense of 'racial ethics' should prevent us from displaying our equals in zoos." In trying to refute this criticism, Virchow weakly insists on the validity of his scientific interest, grounding it in the popular: "everybody… wants to be informed about our position within nature and our evolution" (270). As such, Virchow's article is a demonstration of scientific racism's dilemma to scientifically substantiate its pertinence outside an imperialist and racist socio-political agenda.

Public reactions seem to confirm Virchow's claim. Crowds of people came to see the eight from Labrador, and their visit was popular enough for free enterprise to capitalize on it.

Their presence was used to advertise warm winter clothing, and newspapers reported widely about them. As today, journalistic quality varied from paper to paper, but most of them show a eurocentric and condescending attitude, presenting the Inuit as naïve or child-like creatures. The perceptual frame of most newspaper reporters dictated the stereotypes they presented. In accordance with popular notions about North America's noble but dying "savages" they constructed the Inuit as a "dying race." They catered to the sensational when they reported that a polar bear at the zoo housing the Inuit became very excited by their appearance and recognized the Inuit as its "natural enemies." They appealed to the emotional when they gave a detailed report of Tobias' fondness for children, and their fondness of him. Some of the more sophisticated papers, such as the *Frankfurter Zeitung*, had the more scholarly ethnographic interest in mind and provided more detailed background information. Undoubtedly, Virchow's defence of ethnology, though not the scientific validation he aimed at, was justified: "everybody" wanted to know about the Inuit.

But not everybody was content with objectifying the guests from Labrador into specimens on par with the other specimen exhibited in zoos. J.K's witty and wryly satirical account, which incited Virchow to make his weak public disclaimer, shows an enlightened and above all humane perception, which betrays sensitivity towards and empathy with the objects of the popular and scientific gaze, a perception that is sadly missing in other reports. In the concluding paragraph of her/his article, J.K. sums up the ethical qualms shared by a more humanely inclined section of the public:

Now we would maintain that nothing is gained by the most meticulous observation of all these "interesting details," even when seen from the so-called anthropological point of view. Neither our education nor our knowledge have been expanded or deepened in any way. We cannot, however, and nor can many others, suppress a feeling of embarrassment about these recently proliferating "human exhibitions," and especially about "human exhibitions" in zoological gardens! … If these "interesting" human specimens need to be exhibited at all, a sense of "racial ethics" should prevent us from displaying our equals in zoos. It should be easy to identify appropriate localities elsewhere.

J.K's voice may be considered too weak and too isolated to be heard in the excited uproar of popular voices, but by its example it shows, that it was indeed possible to see things differently and to move from a racializing perception to a perception of "others" as brothers and sisters (with small caps) and members of a common "human race," concluding from such an understanding of *humanitas* (fed by the same classics that also fed phrenology), that "a sense of 'racial ethics' should prevent us from displaying our equals in zoos."

For the Moravian Brothers and Sisters who voiced their concerns about the Inuit from Hebron, the threshold to a common *humanitas* seems to have been baptism, especially a baptism that made people into fellow Moravians. We have seen that from the very start, the missionaries were critical of the whole venture. There are several letters and reports documenting how very opposed they were to Jacobsen's attempts to recruit "their" Inuit. They told Jacobsen: "…we absolutely cannot allow our baptized people to be exhibited like wild animals outside in Europe for money."

(Kretschmer, August 20th). This argument is repeated several times. But the Moravian Brethren voiced not the least concerns about exhibiting the heathens from Nakvak. While their trust in Hagenbeck in hindsight seems naïve, their theological interpretation of the tragedy appears cynical.

To contain and yet to gain, in a spiritual, social and even economic sense, seems to have been the Brethrens greatest concern. While they expressed their wish to keep the heathens and the Christians separated – and Jacobsen complied – and while they wanted Abraham and his family to stay away from sinful contacts with Catholics and other denominations as well as from contamination with materialist greed (and learning the tricks of the trade), they were curious at the same time as to whether "the outside" world would perceive a difference between their baptized converts and Terrianiak, Paingo, and Noggasak. Like all such ventures, the Moravian mission also had an economic agenda, with the Brethren trying to minimize costs and maximize income from "their" baptized Brothers and Sisters. But the trip to Europe brought them no gain. Indeed it led to complications and growing insubordination from their charges, who could now compare fur prices in Europe and Labrador. It seemed better to contain and tightly control outside contacts and to keep "their Eskimos" in childlike ignorance and colonial economic dependence. And yet, at the same time they hoped their mission might profit from Abraham's exposure to "better" music in Europe.

After Abraham and his family had left Labrador, the missionaries in Hebron sent recommendations to their European brethren as to how to treat "their Eskimos" over there. Accordingly, while the travellers were in Germany, local Brethren and former missionaries provided social contacts and spiritual consolation for the group, whereas Terrianiak's people were left entirely to their own spiritual and social devices. Throughout, the missionaries/teachers seem to have been troubled by the fear that their pupils might bring shame upon them and disgrace their missionary project. After the Inuit's deaths there are Moravian comments expressing gratitude and relief that Abraham and his family had remained faithful and disciplined to the very end. The pious Brethren seem to have accepted the death of the Inuit as the working of God's providence, or even as God's vengeance for the neophytes'

disobedience to their teachers. Moreover, while lamenting the loss of their Inuit Brethren, the missionaries seem also to have felt a certain degree of relief, since the deaths of Abraham's group would discourage others, who had obediently stayed behind in Newfoundland, from going on a similar venture. Thus, they hoped that the tragic deaths would serve to support missionary discipline and morale at home. Above all, the Brethren seemed glad to be able to wash their hands from all guilt, as the minutes of the elders conference demonstrated only five weeks after the last survivor, Ulrike, had died: "In spite of most urgent pleading Abraham could not be swayed, and therefore they were free of all responsibilities for the consequences." (UAC minutes, February 24th, 1881)

The following letter from Hebron to Herrnhut, published a year after the event in *Missionsblatt aus der Brüdergemeine* (Nr.1, 1882), documents most clearly the Moravians' ambivalent attitude:

Relating to our Eskimos who died last year in Europe it is written from Hebron:

Of course, we never expected at all that the local Eskimos would have to pay with their lives for their undertaking; that they would become homesick, Ulrike had already predicted. We are glad *(lieb ist es uns!)*, because one day everything had to become so serious that Abraham would see his mistake and feel ashamed of it.

Last winter, when there was great poverty, we were often thankful that Abraham did not stay here for our sake. How often would we have had to hear that he had rejected such high profits because of the teachers and that he now had to suffer together with them. The easiest way for us would always be to let the Eskimos live according to their own will. Abraham was our best violin player at church, and we will miss him a lot. We hoped he would profit from Germany, for his own and for our benefit, because he would hear good music for the first time.

Now the Lord decided according to His own will and placed the homesick-ones in a better land, saved them from sin and earthly misery, and at the same time taught the locals – the ones lusting for Europe – a lesson; because if they had come back healthy and rich, the craving to go to Europe and to grow rich there would have become an epidemic among the other Eskimos. Many of them, who were looking at Abraham and his companions in envy last year, are now silent and happy not to have gone with them.

Since Herr Hagenbeck, and in spite of his big losses, paid all earnings honestly, the relatives of the deceased received the commendable sum of 1120 M. Unfortunately, suspicion is on the rise and is fomented maliciously by people who were not even involved, maintaining that, besides the suitcase of the deceased arrived from Hamburg – which, as a precaution we had opened immediately on the beach in presence of the helmsman and the Eskimos – another bag had arrived containing belongings of Abraham and Tobias. People believe to have learned this from the captain or the helmsman; there is also talk about 5000 Marks, which they are supposed to have earned. Referring to this, and according to what the crewmembers tell them from the newspapers, they draw their own conclusions; when they hear that thousands came to see them in just one day, they think that all of the money thus taken had belonged to their countrymen.

Now, as everybody knows, Eskimos are not the greatest people at numerical systems or the art of calculation, and so it makes no difference to them if you multiply a number by 4 or 5. But, in spite of their clean conscience, this suspicion hurts our Brothers, and they have to leave it to the Lord to vindicate them in the hearts of the people. For themselves, unfortunately, this conviction is also a great misfortune. Despite all the things that happened it would not be impossible, that, if they were asked again next year to go to Europe, some would again let themselves be seduced by the hope of becoming rich.

Individual Brethren, who knew Abraham and met him again in Europe, express their heartfelt personal grief but also their trust in divine providence. The missionaries at Hebron were vindicated: The Lord had punished Abraham for his disobedience, and providence had shown that "the outside" was indeed full of lurking dangers.

Appendix C:
Moravian Mission in Hebron, 2002

Photos by Hans-Ludwig Blohm

Hebron, Moravian Mission, 2002
© *Hans-L. Blohm*

Hebron, 2002
© Hans-L. Blohm

Hebron, Moravian Mission, 2002 © Hans-L. Blohm

*Hebron,
Moravian
Mission,
2002
© Hans-L.
Blohm*

Hebron, Moravian Mission, 2002 © Hans-L. Blohm

Hebron, Moravian Mission, 2002
© *Hans-L. Blohm*

Hebron, Moravian Mission, 2002 © Hans-L. Blohm

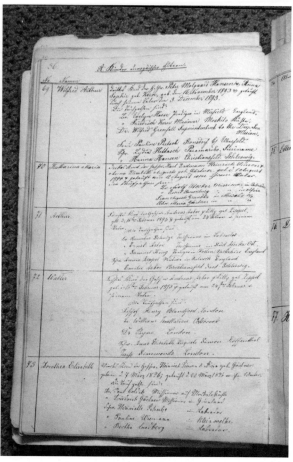

Left: *Local Labrador Inuit Association representative Martha Winter-Abel at Hopedale, Labrador, holding the old Moravian church register from Hebron, March 21, 2002 © Hans-L. Blohm.* **Right:** *Close-up of the Moravian church register from Hebron © Hans-L. Blohm.*

Polar Bear swimming in Ramah Bay, 2002 © Hans-L. Blohm.

Bibliography

Bataille, Gretchen M., and Kathleen Mullen Sands, eds. *American Indian Women Telling Their Lives*. Lincoln: University of Nebraska Press, 1984.

Blohm, Hans-Ludwig. *The Voice of the Natives: The Canadian North and Alaska*. Manotick, Ontario: Penumbra Press, 2001.

Campbell, Lydia. *Sketches of Labrador Life*. (Written in 1894 and published in the *St. John's Evening Telegram*, later edited by her great-great-granddaughter Doris Saunders, publisher of *Them Day* magazine) Grand Falls, Newfoundland: Robinson-Blackmore, 1980.

Feest, Christian D., ed. *Indians and Europe: An Interdisciplinary Collection of Essays*. Lincoln and London: University of Nebraska Press, 1999.

Freeman, Minnie Aodla. *Life Among the Qallunaat*. Edmonton: Hurtig, 1978.

Goudie, Elizabeth. *Woman of Labrador*. Ed. and intr. David Zimmerly. Toronto: Peter Martin Associates, 1973.

Hagenbeck, Carl. *Von Tieren und Menschen: Erlebnisse und Erfahrungen*. Berlin-Ch.: Vita Deutsches Verlagshaus, 1909.

Harper, Kenn. *Give Me My Father's Body: The Life of Minik, the New York Eskimo*. New York: Washington Square Press, 2001.

Herz-Fischler, Roger. *Adolph Zeising: The Life and Work of a German Intellectual*. Ottawa: Mzinhigan Publishing, 2004.

Jacobsen, Adrian. "Translation of the diary kept by Captain Johan Adrian Jacobsen on board the Salleas Eisbaer, 1880," translation by Hedwig Brueckner, Centre for Newfoundland Studies, Memorial University Library, St. John's Newfoundland, unpublished.

Johnston, Basil. "One Generation from Extinction." *Native Writers and Canadian Writing*, ed. W. H. New. Vancouver: University of British Columbia Press, 1990: 10-15.

Jütting, Renate. *Das Tragebuch des Abraham als Beispiel erster Inuit–Literatur*. Hausarbeit im Rahmen der ersten Staatsprüfung für das Lehramt and Realschulen im Lande Niedersachsen. Universität Osnabrück 1991, unpubl.

Lutz, Hartmut. *Approaches: Essays in Native North American Studies and Literatures*. Beiträge zur Kanadistik 11. Augsburg: Wissner, 2002.

———— "'Okay, I'll be their annual Indian for next year': Thoughts on the Marketing of a Canadian Indian Icon in Germany." *Imaginary (Re-)Locations: Tradition, Modernity, and the Market in Contemporary Native American Literature and Culture*. Ed. Helmbrecht Breinig. Tübingen: Stauffenburg Verlag, 2003: 217-245.

———— "Unfit for the European Environment: The Tragedy of Abraham and Other Inuit from Labrador in Hagenbeck's Völkerschau, 1880/81." *Canadian Environments: Essays in Culture, Politics, and History*. Eds. Robert C. Thomsen and Nanette L. Hale. Nordic Association of Canadian Studies Texts 22. Aarhus: University of Aarhus English Dept, 2004: 21 pp. t.b.p.

McGrath, Robin. *Canadian Inuit Literature: The Development of a Tradition*. Canadian Ethnology Service Paper No. 94. Ottawa: National Museums of Canada, 1984.

Nuligak (Bob Cockney). *I, Nuligak*. Ed. and transl. Maurice Metayer. Illus. Ekootak. Markham, Ont.: Simon and Schuster, 1971.

Petrone, Penny. *Northern Voices: Inuit Writing in English*. Toronto: University of Toronto Press, 1988.

Peyer, Bernd C. *The Tutor'd Mind: Indian Missionary-Writers in Antebellum America*. Amherst: University of Massachusetts Press, 1997.

Pitseolak. *Pitseolak: Pictures out of My Life*. Ed. Dorothy Eber. Montreal: Design Collaborative Books; Toronto: Oxford University Press, 1978.

Pitseolak, Peter. *People from Our Side: A Life Story*. Photographs Peter Pitseolak. Oral Biography Dorothy Eber. Edmonton: Hurtig, 1975.

Rivard, Ron, and Catherine Littlejohn. *The History of the Métis of Willow Bunch*. Saskatoon: © Ron Rivard and Catherine Littlejohn, 2003.

Rose, Wendy. "Julia." *Bone Dance: New and Selected Poems 1965–1993*. Tucson: University of Arizona Press, 1994: 60-62.

Taylor, J. Garth. "An Eskimo abroad, 1880: His diary and death." *Canadian Geographic*: 101.5 (Oct./Nov. 1981): 38-43.

Thrasher, Anthony Apakark. *Thrasher ... Skid Row Eskimo*. Toronto: Griffin Press, 1976.

Ulrikab, Abraham. *Tagebuch des Hebroner Eskimos Abraham von seinem Aufenthalt in Europa 1880, übersetzt von Br. Kretschmer*. Unpubl. manuscript.

Virchow, Rudolf. "Ausserordentliche Zusammenkunft im Zoologischen Garten am 7. November 1880. Eskimos von Labrador." *Zeitschrift für Ethnologie* 12 (1880): 253-274.

Hartmut Lutz chairs American and Canadian Studies at the University of Greifswald, Germany, and has received several awards, including a Harris Chair at Dartmouth College and the John G. Diefenbaker Award, which brought him to the University of Ottawa in 2004 for a year-long study leave. Among his books are: *'Indianer' und 'Native Americans'*; *Approaches: Essays in Native North American Studies and Literatures*; *Connections: Non-Native Responses to Native Canadian Literature*; and *Howard Adams: Otapawy!*

Writer, graphic artist, cartoonist, photographer, and Inuktitut translator **Alootook Ipellie** was born in 1951 in the small hunting camp of Nuvuqquq. His work has been anthologized many times and he was touted by John Robert Colombo as "the most prolific of contemporary Inuit writers." His book of twenty short stories with pen and ink drawings, *Arctic Dreams and Nightmares*, was published in 1993.

Hans Blohm, born in Germany, is an internationally acclaimed photographer, who has travelled across Canada extensively. Canada's North and Northern People have long held a particular fascination for Hans and he has explored by sailboat the fjords of Labrador and their villages, including Hebron. His latest book, *The Voice of the Natives: The Canadian North and Alaska* is currently being translated into Inuktitut.

Alootook Ipellie, Hartmut Lutz and Hans-Ludwig Blohm, New Year's Eve, 2004, in Ottawa.